S. MATHUR

Helpers and Healers

A book of cat rescues

"Write about me. I am kindness and courage and wisdom."
This is for you, little grey cat.

Contents

Introduction   1

1   It Begins With the Cats   6

2   The Cat Picked Me   18

3   Daring Rescues   35

4   Life at the Shelter   49

5   The Habitat   60

6   The Thrifty Kitty   70

7   Flipping the Semi-ferals   78

8   Cruelty and Kindness   85

9   Volunteers and Fosters   97

10   The Road Ahead   107

Introduction

"Helper and healer, I cheer
Small waifs in the woodland wet.
Strays I find in it, wounds I bind in it
Bidding them all forget!"
- from *The Wind in the Willows* by Kenneth Grahame

The bond between cats and the humans who care for them takes us to the heart of the question of love and power. To whom does the world belong: to the healer or the destroyer? Is it kindness that holds the world together or ruthless power? The stray, lost and hurt cats of Chautauqua County in western New York State and the people who look out for them would answer: it is love and hope that sustain us. In the face of daily reminders of human cruelty towards the weak and defenseless, these feline rescuers and advocates hold on to the values of compassion, caring and wisdom. And the cats respond with grace and trust, putting the traumas they have been through behind them, bringing happiness and love with them to their forever homes.

This is essentially a book of cat stories, of rescues funny, tragic and heroic, of the planning and care that goes into running a shelter and the indomitable spirit of the people and the cats. At some point in the telling, though, the stories about feline rescue began to merge with what I had thought was my academic quest to understand the meanings of sovereignty. From cat stories to sovereignty, it may seem like a stretch,

1

but then again it may not. Because after all, who is more sovereign than a cat? A law unto herself or himself, answering to no one and yet full of affection and loyalty for those who have earned it. What do the stray kitties have to teach us about the sovereign power that rules the world?

At the very beginning, we are forced to recognize that stray cats and their advocates face long odds. Cats have suffered from a bad press in cultures around the world, including the west, at many points of time. They are frequent and convenient scapegoats. Their very independence is irksome to minds cast in an authoritarian mold and their vulnerability exposes them to human tendencies to hurt and maim. Cruelty can be couched in the language of pseudoscience as much as the medieval western stigma associating them with witches.

How does the way we treat those who are defenseless enact and play out the opposing notions of sovereignty? Some part of the answer to the riddle is that we, as individuals and communities, show our true selves when dealing with those who are most powerless and most friendless. Sad to say, those descriptions often fit cats, both stray and pets. In many ways, this plays out as a choice between two paths we can take through the world - to destroy or to heal. As these feline rescue stories show, this is where we can see humans at their worst and also at their best. Why does it matter that some people are cruel to animals and that others are kind?

There is a well-established body of empirical evidence, from the fields of law enforcement and research on psychopathy, that traces the direct connection between cruelty to animals and violent crimes against humans. Records show that some of the most notorious psychopaths and serial killers started out as animal abusers before moving on to human targets. In 2016, the FBI added the crime of animal cruelty to its national database in 2016, making it a felony crime like arson, burglary, assault and homicide. A setting where animal cruelty is happening is also likely a setting for domestic violence and child abuse. Animal cruelty is not only a gateway crime but a red flag. There is a continuity in how we humans treat each other and the natural world. There is no clear demarcation between the two, despite the insistence of many religious and cultural traditions.

When looking at political violence, environmental devastation and cruelty to animals, the notion of sovereignty as unchecked power becomes the linking factor: the way we treat animals, and the natural world is a reflection of the way we treat each other. We've all been talking and hearing for years about how our modes of living are destroying the environment. At this point, it's clear that this process is almost complete, and the question is more one of whether recovery and healing are possible. But if human and animal hurts go together, so do human and animal weal. What would healing the world look like? Can we "save" or restore the environment while continuing with endless destructive wars? Can we respect the "Rights of Nature" without also respecting the rights of animals?

The answer I'm working towards may be phrased like this: If the different forms of harm, against animals, humans and the environment, are interconnected, so must the forms of healing be connected. There is not a separate notion of human sovereignty over nature and animals that is distinct from the political notion of sovereignty. We are all inextricably bound in the great web of life, with the choice to do harm or to do good.

In the end, the answers are very simple. We've even known them for a long time. What's difficult is the doing. It takes kindness, but also courage and wisdom. Feline rescue is part of the answer, a nexus of good where people come together to help these beautiful, intelligent creatures caught up in varied misfortunes. This book is about people and cats who show us on a daily basis the power of love, hope and courage. To me, it sounds like a message for our times.

The book was written over a couple of years from 2016 to 2018 and the events it covers should be read as a record of those days. Karen Hubbard was at that time director of the Westfield Stray Cat Rescue, putting in more than forty hours every week, on a voluntary basis, to keep the Shelter running and the cats healthy and happy. There was a large team of volunteers, who made the Shelter and its associated store, the Thrifty Kitty, a cheerful and welcoming place.

As everywhere in the world following the pandemic, much has changed at the Shelter and in people's lives. The store was forced to close for over six months and the number of volunteers dropped. Due to ill health, Karen had to pull back from her work at the Shelter and focus on the Habitat for difficult-to-adopt cats at her home. But the Shelter continues its work and Karen continues to care for the cats that have nowhere else to go and no one else to look out for them.

Chatterbox is a helper and healer too

1

It Begins With the Cats

Everybody knows that cats are plotting to take over the world. In fact, they've already taken over the Internet. But we humans needn't worry: the cats will be benevolent dictators. Everyone will get to play as well as work and no one will go to bed hungry. But until that day, all of us, humans and cats, live in a world that is full of mischance and accident. And contrary to all our ideas of right and wrong, it's often the good, the innocent and the weak who suffer most from these misfortunes, whether these are accidental or deliberately created. Animals come in for more than their share of trouble, in a world made by and for humans with little or no concern for their welfare. Not only is the human-made world full of dangers for animals, but domesticated animals like cats and dogs are easy and frequent targets for deliberate cruelty.

And yet, many of us find it difficult to face the reality of cruelty to animals and try to avoid accounts of stray, lost and mistreated cats and dogs, for a number of reasons. It's easier to look away. These stories produce a number of strong emotions: helplessness, because there's often very little to nothing you can do to help; anger, at those who carry out the abuse and get away with it; sadness and horror at the cruelty inflicted on helpless and innocent creatures. It is in their interactions with the weak, the injured and the helpless that we often see humans at their worst. The contrast between deliberate cruelty and its innocent victims awakens a deep horror in our hearts.

But there's much more to animal rescue stories. They also show humans at their best. This is a book about those who turn their sadness and anger into a vocation of kindness and caring. Feline rescuers are driven by the bond between cats and humans, inexplicable and deep-rooted. It takes courage, kindness, wisdom and faith to persist on this difficult path. The rewards are intangible, but precious, as frightened and hurt felines recover their cheerfulness and courage and find a place for themselves in their forever homes.

The first seed of the idea for this book was planted when I met Karen Hubbard through the Westfield Stray Cat Rescue (WSCR) back in 2013. I was desperately looking for homes for five kittens someone had abandoned in the woods and calling every shelter and animal rescue within a fifty-mile radius. The full story of the kittens of Forestville is told in Chapter 8, but here it's enough to say that in the end Karen and the WSCR came through for me. They offered to pay the fees for the veterinary examination - with five kittens and very little spare cash that was a very big help. Karen then offered to take in and foster the smallest, a tiny black kitten who had a hard time recovering from the ordeal.

Karen's "can-do" attitude and the welcoming feel of the shelter and store were like a lifeline in a very difficult situation. They were also quite different from my earlier experiences of shelters, where workers tend to be overworked and caged animals are crowded up to each other and stressed out. In sharp contrast, WSCR was a cheerful, upbeat place with cheerful, upbeat people and cats who were loved and recognized as individuals. This is not at all to disparage the work of busy shelters in large cities and more heavily populated areas, which inevitably also have a larger population of strays. Shelter workers around the world are incredibly dedicated and kind people, working against huge odds. But the shelter in Westfield could be a model for the future, with more of the feel of a home and playroom than a combined prison and hospital.

Over time, as I sat down and talked with Karen and other volunteers about the shelter and its work, I slowly began to see the story behind the stories. The book about their rescue work became entangled with what I thought was quite a different project, my own search for understanding the sources of human cruelty and kindness. Why are some people kind and why do others actively work to hurt other living creatures? What is the meaning, if there is one, of the juxtaposition of cruelty with kindness and beauty? What is the way forward?

Chautauqua, that magical corner of western New York State, is for many reasons a place where I thought there might be answers. And in the work done by Karen and other feline rescuers, I began to find some of those answers. Injured, homeless, stray and abandoned cats and kittens were brought to them by their traumatized human rescuers and taken in with a smile and kind words. They are given hugs, both cats and people, and the cats get medical care, food and love before being sent off to their ideal forever homes, healed and happy. I had thought the great mystery of the world was the cruelty we encounter here, but I found that even greater is the mystery of kindness.

The relationship between humans and cats is a deep and ancient one, affirmed in societies around the world. In good times and bad, there have always been people who have done their best to care for these intriguing, graceful animals. This bond reminds us that we humans belong to the natural world, despite all that we have done to destroy it. And the cats, in their turn, give us their complex gifts of playfulness, dignity, beauty and courage. The world of cat rescue brings out all the richness of the human-feline relationship. However, for some reason, shelter and rescue stores haven't been told as widely as have other cat stories.

I was lucky enough to get a close-up view of the rescue, the people, the cats and the community that sustains them. To all of them and to the volunteer staff, I am deeply grateful for taking the time out of their busy schedules and lives to help me understand the world of cat rescue and shelters. And for trusting me, a complete stranger, to tell their stories. As often happens, the stories wrote themselves - funny, sad, hopeful. Cat lovers can never get enough of them. It was only slowly that I came to see the profound meanings and patterns behind them. The cats and the people who care for them have so much to teach us about the power of love and hope to heal wrongs. This is the message we all need to hear right now.

Karen Hubbard generously gave me hours of her time and shared her experiences, knowledge of the shelter and its history and working and cat stories. Likewise, Celeste Kerns and Judy Loomis, the founders of WSCR and former members of the Board of Directors, took the time to talk to me despite their multiple commitments. Celeste met with me on several occasions, over meals, a church potluck and at the tenth-anniversary celebration of the shelter and store. At one of those meetings, she gave me her copy of the weekly service schedule from her church, with a verse from Isaiah (32:18): "My people shall dwell in a peaceful habitation and in sure dwellings and in quiet resting places." It came to me later that it was the perfect wish for all creatures in troubled times.

The cats are helpers and healers too, as every cat person knows. WSCR shelter cats are a cheerful and loving lot, with unique personalities that reflect the love and care they receive. Most of them have been through traumas that the humans who care for them will never know about. But they bounce back with a mixture of grace, dignity and playfulness that are lessons in themselves. The staff and volunteers are likewise cheerful and upbeat and utterly dedicated to the furry little beasts. If cats are indeed, as many believe, genii loci or the spirits of the place, Westfield NY is in good hands. Or paws.

The little black kitten who was abandoned in the woods of Forestville and taken in by Karen recovered and found a good home.

November 4, 2016

Fallon watched over us as we talked. I was meeting with Karen in the shelter office, to learn the story of WSCR. Fallon is a large, calm tiger calico with a few white patches and a white front and paws, very comfortable in her role as the office cat. She added a few views and mews of her own, knocked a mug full of pens off the desk and then, satisfied that all was well, retreated to her cat condo for a well-earned nap.

I'd met Karen a few times before, almost each time in a crisis connected with abandoned or sick kittens. Each time, she has been an angel of mercy, taking them in with a smile and a welcome. And each time, she has performed miracles, healing the little ones and finding them loving homes. The Shelter, its people and the Thrifty Kitty, the thrift store that supports the shelter, act as a magnet, an oasis of goodness, calm, friendly felines and vintage bargains. It feels like magic, good magic. But to make it happen takes a lot of hard work, planning and cooperation.

While visitors see the surface calm, days at the shelter can be chaotic and demanding, Karen tells me. Especially in the summer, when the largest number of kittens are born, things can get crazy. What inspires her to keep going are some of the people and how they will go out of their way to help cats. Even when they don't have a lot of money, they make a big effort to help the creatures in distress. That effort can mean so much, for them, the cats and the shelter. She recalled a young man who recently brought in a tiny kitten that he found hiding in his yard; it had been frightened by his dog. He rescued her and brought her into WSCR because he didn't have the money to pay for gas to drive her the extra thirty miles to the Humane Society in Jamestown. Because he had so little, but still chose to help the kitten, his effort was the equivalent of hundreds of dollars.

"To see the caring," Karen says, "And the cats and how they touch people's hearts. So much of it is about the people and the kinds of trouble they go to help cats and bring them to us." Sometimes the rescuers can be the least likely people. She tells me about another recent addition to the shelter, a tiny grey kitten who was brought in by a truck driver. He found her by the roadside with her feet tied up in duct tape. He told Karen that when he first saw her, he just drove past, thinking "Is that your problem? No, that is not your problem." He couldn't stop thinking about the kitten, however and a little way down the road, he said to himself: "I guess it is my problem," and turned around. He brought her into the shelter holding her against his heart. The little grey kitten went to a good home, to a family with kids.

11

What makes animal rescue stories so inspiring are the people who have dedicated themselves to rescuing injured and stray animals. And of course, it's about the cats. Each cat is an individual and the challenge is to understand what they have to tell us. Cats are great survivors, Karen says, though they don't get the credit they deserve for it. She's certainly seen enough cat survivors to speak with authority on the subject. They can adapt and change according to the environment they're in; they can also, as Karen has helped them do so many times, overcome all kinds of trauma and disability to lead happy and fulfilling lives.

As I learned more and more about the shelter and all the collaboration, hard work and organization it takes, I started to wonder what the cats make of WSCR and its people. Cats are highly intelligent and also highly opinionated. What do they think of these humans who move heaven and earth to help their fellow felines in distress? How do they regard the shelter? They surely communicate with each other about it all: the volunteers, the visitors, the kids, the food, the toys. But being cats, they won't give us humans a direct answer. The Cheshire Cat in the Alice books is the perfect example of the propensity of cats for riddles and jokes upon hapless humans lost in strange worlds. We have to work it out for ourselves.

Working at WSCR has changed her too, Karen feels. Diplomacy is not her strong suit but at the shelter, she finds that a lot of the time, she's being the diplomat, pulling people together to work for the cats. "I'm an outspoken person. I've learned to be diplomatic because the cats need us all to work together. It's having a purpose that's larger than ourselves," she said, "Cats are my purpose. My needs and wants don't matter." When she's feeling less diplomatic, too, the cats have an answer. Karen's family and the shelter staff are familiar with her 'channeling' the cats' demands for more food, faster and cleaner litter boxes, as well as their frank comments on some of the goings-on in the store.

So many cats and so many stories. And while there are many success stories, there are also the sad ones about cats and kittens that were too sick or badly injured to live. How do Karen and her colleagues find the courage to keep going? What about the ones that don't end well? How do you deal with the sadness and not give up? "My faith is very strong," she says. Dr. Rogers, who used to work at the Village Veterinary Clinic and has recently retired, helped WSCR for years and was a great support. He always said that we do what we can to help them. For those we lose, God surely has a plan, says Karen. Sometimes they are too sick or badly injured to save, but instead of being out there all alone, cold, frightened, lonely and possibly injured, they're with people who love them.

The shelter interacts with the community in many different ways, through rescues, adoptions, special events, and a popular thrift store. Running a shelter takes organization and planning and also a healthy amount of hope and faith. Karen feels that she and the shelter keep going because help arrives when it's needed. In fact, she believes that help will be given when it's needed. She recalled a time a few years back when they were trying to raise funds and the money was needed quite desperately. The shelter operates on a shoestring budget and any extra money immediately goes to new projects. In this context, Karen goes by a friend's advice on running a non- profit, that it's not a good idea to be sitting on a huge bank account. Any extra funds should go into growing the work of the organization.

On that occasion, the Bob Evans restaurant in Dunkirk was helping WSCR with fundraising, by donating fifteen percent of the cost of each meal when diners brought in a flyer from the shelter. Karen was with some volunteers outside the restaurant, handing out flyers to people as they walked in. Just then, a tour bus from Texas pulled up outside, full to the seams with diners and animal lovers. Priscilla Marsh, co-director of WSCR who was at the restaurant with Karen, saw this as divine intervention on behalf of the stray kitties: "If that isn't direct proof that the Good Lord loves cats, I don't know what is."

A Quiet Place

For any writer, the two essentials are to find the story and to find the voice in which to tell the story. With cats and rescues, there were plenty of stories. The problem was to find the right voice in which to tell them. I had originally thought of writing an official biography of the shelter, but it kept turning into a record of my own idiosyncratic journey of understanding. For some reason, my life keeps bringing me back to Chautauqua. I had driven through and past before, many times, along I-90 on the way from Massachusetts to Ohio and back, not stopping but sensing and seeing the difference without understanding it. Entering the profound silence of Cattaraugus and Chautauqua counties, there is also a subtle visual shift, clearly discernible but difficult to describe, setting it apart from every other place I have seen in the US.

Chautauqua is, to me, the Place of the Trees, defined by Lakes Erie and Chautauqua. It's not just the size of the trees, but the sense that this is their domain, where they can live and grow freely. Their very shapes and the shape of the land itself, seem to be free of human interference. Perhaps it's because this is still Iroquois country, where the reservations hold on to the spirit of a different way of understanding the natural world. It hasn't been clipped and manicured and domesticated within an inch of its life. The woods preserve their undergrowth, the very grass verges speak of a land that has not yet been brought under human management.

I had discovered early on that I wasn't alone in thinking of Chautauqua as a special place. It has been a magnet for utopians and mystics, truth seekers of one kind or another, for a long time. Two of the county's most famous institutions - the Chautauqua Institution and Lily Dale - embody this quest. My own personal search for understanding the beauty and terror of life itself kept bringing me back here to face harsh and inescapable questions, about the nature of goodness and evil.

And then there's the simple fact that there's magic in the air. Over the years, I've tried to rationalize it, finally deciding that it lies in the quality of the silence. It's the vast scale of human absence that gives it a peaceful, magical air, of a place set apart from the world. But magic can be both good and bad and in all the stories I've read, it comes with testing times.

I first came here to finish a book manuscript, the record of my research on human rights abuses in a conflict zone. And in the quiet upland woods and meadows of Forestville, I learned that my book was also about the courage of the survivors. I learned that while claims to sovereignty can be based on absolute power, there are also the opposing and equally powerful claims of love, justice, courage and hope. I learned that the outcome of the contest between the two claims is not yet decided. Indeed, our own actions may help decide the outcome. Chautauqua had worked its magic, bringing understanding and healing. But the place wasn't finished with me yet.It had to show me how it was done.

As I kept returning to Chautauqua over the years, I watched Karen and WSCR volunteers take in rescues, care for them at the shelter and reach out to the community at farmers markets and other events. I heard about their trap neuter return (TNR) program every summer for feral cats, or community cats as some feline advocates prefer to call them. I met the volunteers who run the shelter and The Thrifty Kitty, the store that helps fund WSCR. Over time it became clear to me that this is the power of love and hope in action, channeled and directed. Underlying all of this is the spirit of cheerful optimism of which there seems to be an endless well in the community. I had, finally, run out of questions.

––––

Karen mentioned in the beginning that people think that a shelter is a calm, cozy place and all one needs to do is spend time playing with adorable kittens. There's that, of course, but as the stories of cats rescued from ill-treatment show, WSCR staff and volunteers come face to face every day with the cruelty, pain and hardship these beautiful creatures have to face. Underlying the kindness there is a resolve, a determination to not flinch from the sadness they encounter in rescue work every day. Sometimes the pain is due to an accident, illness, or misfortune, at other times the cruelty is actively planned and carried out by humans. I doubt that I would have the courage that Karen and Celeste and the people at WSCR do, to face this every day and to still keep on track helping cats and kittens in distress to live their best possible lives.

Taking to Karen reminded me of something I had read a while ago, about the cats of the Hermitage Museum in St. Petersburg. The Museum used to be the Winter Palace of the Tzars and is home to some of the great artistic treasures of the world. Since 1745, it has also been home to numerous cats, who are officially designated as staff. The cats are a visitor attraction in themselves and before they were put on the payroll, Museum staff would bring them food out of their own limited budgets.

The official role of the cats is to catch mice, but they really don't kill that many. In fact, they hardly see any mice, since their very presence acts as a deterrent to pests. Speaking of their importance, the official responsible for their well-being said in an interview that it was good to have the cats around because "They bring out the best in humans."

It begins with the cats, Karen says, and expands to include the entire community.

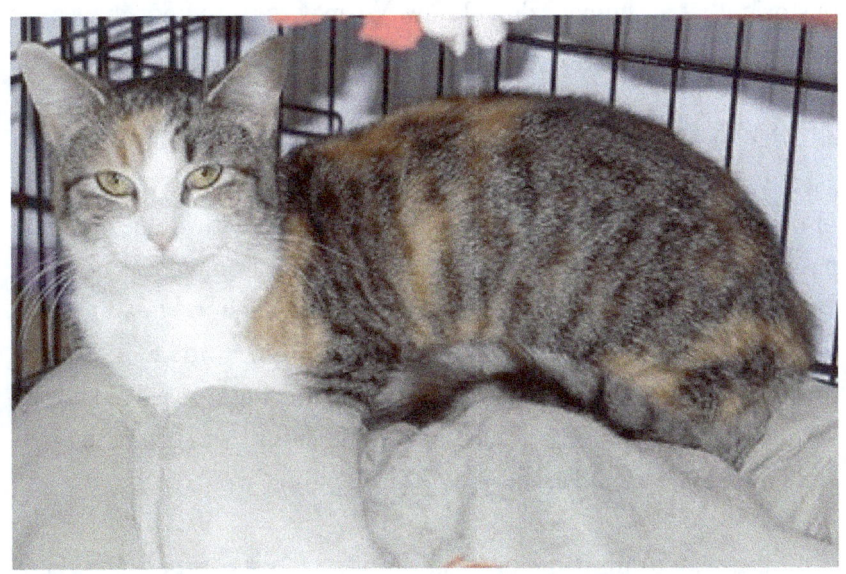

Fallon, the office cat, relaxing in her cat condo. November 2016

2

The Cat Picked Me

Where there's a cat, there's a story. In fact, there are probably all kinds of stories that we humans don't know. We may come to know how a cat was found, or rescued, or brought to a forever home. We'll never know much about their lives before and the hardships and fears they faced and that's only partly because they can't talk to us in words. Cats have a gift for transcending their sufferings, carrying on with the business of life in a spirit of grace and playfulness that gives few clues to their past hardships. That's certainly the case with Fallon, who is now the Office Cat at WSCR and a senior member of the shelter. She was found during a TNR or Trap Neuter Return operation in the neighboring town of Ripley. She was one of several cats living in a disused old tavern building. The owner of the house behind the tavern was trying to catch and home the cats and asked WSCR to help him.

TNR is a way to limit the population of stray cats and to help them live a better life. It does exactly what it says, but a bare description of the process doesn't describe the hours of anxiety and care involved in humanely trapping feral cats. Many people who do TNR will leave traps out overnight, but Karen and WSCR volunteers never leave one unwatched. The dangers to the cats, from predators and humans, are too great if they are left trapped and defenseless. Also, the cats are naturally upset at being trapped, but if someone is watching, the trap can be covered with a towel or cloth, which calms them down. For many shelters, TNR has become a major part of their mission to help stray and feral cats, as it helps to reduce their population in the area. Fewer strays means a lower potential for accidents and a reduced burden on overcrowded shelters, making it a most humane solution. Shelters around the country report a drop in intakes when TNR projects are started in their area. Once caught, cats are kept for about a week before being returned back to their homes. During that time they are spayed or neutered, vaccinated and given any other veterinary treatments needed.

When they are returned back into their familiar habitats, they settle down quickly. Some critics of TNR object to releasing cats back into their habitat, given the potential dangers of outdoor life. However, kittens and any grown cats that can be tamed or 'flipped,' are never released back into the wild, but are adopted out. It is only the true ferals, who are made miserable by human contact and who are well adapted to their environments, that are returned back. Some ferals are lucky enough to find homes as farm and barn cats. Fallon was one of the semi-ferals who could be tamed. So she stayed at the shelter, putting her life as a tavern wench, as Karen calls it, behind her.

When Tilly finally left for her own home, the post of office cat fell vacant. Tilly was a pastel tortoiseshell with grey and tan fur, who had an aversion to anyone who wanted to adopt her. She would start out being aloof, but if that didn't work, she would hiss and scratch. Karen recalls with amusement the look on Tilly's face when confronting a human who wanted nothing more than to take her home and look after her for the rest of their lives. Until the day came and with it the right person. Tilly changed her demeanor completely, became friendly and cuddly and went to her forever home with an artist and crafter. And that was how Fallon became the office cat. Tilly, it is reported, is doing well and rules the house.

For a few months, Fallon shared the office with Frankie Boy. Frankie Boy's story is a sobering reminder of the vulnerability of cats to the whims and random cruelty of humans. He had been adopted from WSCR as a kitten, but years later, when he was thirteen, things changed for the worse with his family. The wife passed away and the father and daughter were moving to Florida and decided not to take the cat with them. The father called WSCR to ask them to take the Frankie Boy in. Failing that, he said, the cat would have to be euthanized. Karen has encountered this situation twice when owners threatened to euthanize their cats if they could not give them up to WSCR. Both times, her answer was the same: she would take the cat, provided the owner made a donation to the shelter for the same amount as the cost of euthanasia. Both times, the owners agreed to make the donation.

So Frankie Boy came back to WSCR but due to his age and ill health, he was difficult to adopt. But then his day came too and with it, his person: a professor at the College at Fredonia. And they lived happily ever after.

Fallon now presides over the office and takes her responsibilities as a senior member of the shelter very seriously. It has been difficult for her to be adopted because she has trouble with her paws, which have a tendency to develop sores. She has lived at WSCR since 12/30/13, according to her file folder. WSCR maintains excellent records and each cat has a file folder with details of dates, medical treatments and conditions and adoption. Fallon shows no traces of her feral past, being very social and friendly and also very vocal, not to say bossy.

She was adopted out once but didn't do so well in her new home and eventually came back to the shelter to resume her duties as office cat. Tami, one of the most dedicated WSCR volunteers, felt that she missed Buster, her office-mate. Buster is a shy black cat who lives in the office, because he has to be kept apart from the other cats except Fallon. He eats a special diet food and isn't allowed to eat regular cat food. In the adult cats' room, they're all in and out of each other's cat condos all day and being cats, find it so much more fun to eat someone else's food than their own. In the office, it's possible to keep him away from the forbidden food. He still manages to sneak occasional mouthfuls of Fallon's regular food, but she doesn't seem to mind. Tami feels that they will have to be adopted together.

Cats and kittens are ready for their forever homes when they're completely healthy, vaccinated, fixed and properly socialized. They come with their own toys and catnip pillows. Kittens have to be at least eight weeks old before going to their new homes, according to New York State law. In the meantime, they live with foster families and come to the shelter regularly to be socialized with volunteers and meet potential adopters. That means lots of games and cuddling. As a result, cats adopted from the shelter are happy and secure. Whatever pain, hardship and fear they have suffered is now behind them and they are loved and looked after. They know it and they're happy to be there.

Like all shelters, WSCR has an adoption policy which specifies certain conditions that potential adopters have to meet. They have to commit to providing a safe home, healthcare and so on. The adoption fee is $50 for adults or kittens, which is low compared to the fees charged by other shelters and rescue organizations. Judy recalls that in the beginning, WSCR didn't charge an adoption fee for cats. But that didn't work out well; sometimes people wouldn't value the cats they took, or care for them. After a few cats were brought back in bad shape, the policy was changed and an adoption fee of $25 was instituted.

People adopting multiple cats or kittens, or a special needs cat, can pay a special low fee. And those who would like to help a cat to find a home but can't adopt one themselves, for whatever reason, can become Adoption Angels. By making a donation to cover adoption fees, they can help someone who can't afford the fee to give a home to a cat or kitten. Adoption Angels can buy gift certificates at the online Kitty Shack WebStore. There are also Gift Certificates for the Thrifty Kitty Store at the online store.

WSCR is a no-kill shelter, and it does not turn away special needs cats. Special needs felines may have health problems like diabetes, which need extra care and medications. Because of these requirements, they are only adopted to homes that are willing and set up to provide this care. WSCR commits to picking up the tab for medical needs for special needs cats throughout their lives, even when they are in their forever homes. Orphaned kittens and blind cats also have special needs and then there are the ferals who are not fully socialized. Ferals can't really become family pets or even stay indoors. They're not comfortable around humans but will do well in a barn setting or on a farm and luckily there are enough of those in this rural county.

Each cat has different needs when it comes to choosing a home and

WSCR staff put a lot of effort into matching cats their most suitable homes and families. Sometimes finding the right home can just be a matter of chance. Judy recalls a cat that was returned to the shelter because it hated being indoors and would streak out the door the moment it was opened. The house was on a busy street, which made it a dangerous situation for the cat. At exactly the same time when the cat was brought back to WSCR, someone stopped by looking for a cat that could live outdoors. They needed a barn cat to keep away the pests and so the outdoors- seeking cat found the perfect home.

Another abandoned kitten showed me that there is indeed a perfect home waiting for every feline, we just need to find it. This was a small black kitten I found last summer, all alone by herself on a dirt road out in the country. She was completely adorable but turned our household upside down with her antics. After having spent some indeterminate amount of time on her own in the woods, she absolutely did not want to be left alone. She would try and cuddle up to my cat at all times, with me as a second best choice.

Taffy-Cat, I'm sorry to say, while perfectly willing to tolerate other cats at a distance, turned out to be touch-phobic and displayed some very bad temper. I had to lock the kitten or myself in the bathroom to meet work deadlines. She was quick and eager to investigate everything, and some mishaps happened. Paws were caught in closing fridge doors and once I had to retrieve her from inside the washer, luckily not in use that day. Just in the nick of time, Maggie, a lively young woman who lives in the area, saw my posting on Facebook and it turns out that a madcap kitten is exactly what she was looking for. With young children and a friendly cat and dog, the kitten now has plenty of playmates and furry friends to cuddle.

Like all fosters, we love hearing of her progress in her new home. Maggie sends pictures of Pazza, the crazy kitten, now a fearless teen, stealing the dog's bed, sharing the birdwatching window seat curled up with her sister cat, sitting right in the middle of the children's games and investigating the contents of her very own hand-knitted Christmas stocking. The abandoned waif is now safe and happy in the heart of a fun and loving family, with that little touch of magic that accompanies every happy ending.

Cats are good at finding their own forever homes sometimes when they get a chance. That's the story of Cassie, a long-haired calico with a mind of her own who went through several transitions before choosing the home she liked best. She first showed up at a feeding station in a rural corner of northeast Ohio, where an older couple looked after ten outdoor cats, providing them food, water and shelter. They noticed that the new calico was having trouble eating and needed veterinary care. Due to ill health, they were unable to take her to the vet themselves and a neighbor posted a call for help on Facebook.

With winter and the first snow coming on, I was concerned for her and asked my neighbor Mark, a vineyard owner, if he wanted to adopt her. He and his family were cat people and he had been talking about getting a cat for natural pest control. They got along well and Cassie (short for "Cassoulet," since she is three colors) settled in happily, safely out of the cold. She made herself at home, inside and outside the house and soon began going walkabout for days at a time. And then, just before Christmas, she stopped coming home altogether.

Imagining the worst, we searched the neighborhood and asked at all likely houses within a half- mile radius if they had seen Cassie. We had given up hope, but a month later, a helpful suggestion from a missing pets group on Facebook led me to a house that was further than I thought a cat would wander.

This turned out to be the perfect home Cassie had found for herself with Christine, a hidden peaceable kingdom, haven and sanctuary for cats and other creatures. There are chickens and ducks wandering around and corn for deer in the winter when the grazing is sparse. Cassie is well loved and cared for, free to wander the rural paradise all day as she wants and at night she sleeps on a pillow beside her favorite person in all the world.

Luckily, this story has happy endings all around and Mark too was not left without the benefit of feline company for long. Chuck, a vocal, rough-and-tumble tabby with soft grey fur showed up and claimed his own place at the little house on the vineyard.

––––

There's always a need for both foster and forever homes for the special needs felines. The cost of any special medications and treatment is covered by WSCR, even after they go to their foster or forever homes, for the lifetime of the cat. Another condition of adoption for any cat or kitten from WSCR is that if there's ever a time that the owner can't continue to look after the cat, it must be brought back to the shelter.

The cats and even the tiny kittens, of course, have their own ideas about homes and people. It's difficult to escape the idea that they pick their human as much as the humans pick them. And there's no denying that even the tiniest kitten will sometimes reach out a paw and pick a human to take them home and love them forever. You can almost hear the command: "You, human, may take me home, feed me and care for me and fulfill my slightest whim." The lucky humans are those who recognize this command and begin their obedience training early. Celeste feels that people are attracted to the cat or kitten that reaches out to them, as it feels like they are being chosen.

Older cats are more difficult to adopt because everyone wants a kitten. But older cats often make the best pets. They're calm and intelligent and adaptable. Or else they're so good at training humans gently that people don't even realize that their lives are being adapted to the cat's tastes and convenience. Older cats also make good companions for seniors living on their own. More than any others, adult cats know when their humans are feeling low and also exactly how to cheer them up. Likewise, many shelters find that black cats can be difficult to find homes for and they're still the last to be adopted. Shelters are justifiably cautious about giving them to new homes around Halloween. WSCR is exceptional in that there's never been a problem in finding homes for black cats. As a human who has been lucky enough to be owned by two black cats, I know that they are something special. Maybe it's the purity of their color, or their iconic, heraldic appearance. There's definitely a strong element of the guardian angel about them.

Cats and kittens who are ready for their forever homes go to the adoption events, at different locations in Westfield and across Chautauqua County. These adoption events double as fundraisers and are held throughout the year, often hosted by local businesses and institutions. Churches, banks, fire stations, libraries, hairdressers, pet supplies stores and even golf courses: no one can resist the charm of wide open eyes, pointy ears and tiny paws. While the Rules prevent these establishments from opening their doors to cats full-time, they donate space and time to host adoption events and fundraisers. A year-round cycle of events, plus weekly appearances at the Westfield Farmers Market and other community events keeps adoptions going and donations coming in.

Finding the right forever homes for cats and kittens involves communication and interactions with the community, in ways old and new. In the early days of WSCR, there was no shelter building, and the rescued felines were housed as fosters in volunteer homes. Because the cats were in foster homes, there was no place like the shelter where people could go to visit the cats available for adoption. The only way to get the information about cats and kittens who were ready for their forever homes was through strategically-placed flyers around the community: these were the old-fashioned kind of flyers, with the phone number on tear-off tabs at the bottom. The flyers are now supplemented with online communications, which reach a wider audience and are more easily shared.

Through the website, the Facebook page, Amazon and eBay, friends and supporters are kept informed of news, events, details about cats and kittens who need homes, help and supplies needed at the shelter and more. Supporters who shop online at Amazon can also choose WSCR as their designated charity to receive donations with every order. Cats and kittens for adoption are also listed on Petfinder.com, which is an online listing and resource for shelters. The shelter's social media and online stores are maintained by volunteers donating their time and talent.

The biggest annual adoption event is Catapaloosa, which happens every year in May, at the peak time for kittens. WSCR volunteers bring twenty to thirty kittens to the venue, which changes from year to year. The venue is usually a space offered for the event by supporters in the community. The first Catapaloosa was held in 2015, at the West Portland Baptist Church, which has a large indoor space, almost like a pole barn. There are stalls with numerous vendors from the community. Chinese Auction baskets and donated baked goods are popular favorites. And of course, the kittens are the star attraction.

There are other regular events in the community where cats and kittens ready for adoption are introduced to the world. They go to the Westfield Arts and Crafts Festival in July, the Antique Books Show at the end of August and Christmas and Easter events in Westfield and Ripley. Even with the multiple attractions at these events, the WSCR table with its friendly cats and kittens is a huge draw. The "Awwww!" factor kicks in and people's expressions change to happy and even mushy the moment the cats and kittens are sighted. The cats and especially the kittens are happy to be surrounded by a circle of adoring humans, many of them wishing they had room at home for just one more cat. Karen has a priceless opening line to introduce her charges: "These are some specimens of our stray kitties."

However, cats and kittens are not adopted on the spot at any of the events: potential adopters have to fill out an application form and references are checked carefully. There are serious discussions about the needs of the adopter and the cat and cats and kittens are matched to families and homes carefully. The cats and their personalities are well known, and every effort is made to find the right home for everyone.

Is there a pattern to the adoptions? Do they decline during periods of economic hardship? Celeste says that the staff at WSCR have asked themselves the same questions, but it's difficult to find a correlation or to identify any patterns. For example, the first two months of 2015 saw a record number of adoptions, at the rate of one per day. There are times when the number of adoptions falls off and it's difficult if not impossible to pinpoint the causes. What would help, Celeste says, is to have more volunteers who could take cats and kittens to the weekly farmers markets in the summer.

Westfield has been, and still is, all about "the grapes." Part of the Lake Erie wine country, it is surrounded by vineyards and was the national headquarters of the Welch Food Company. The company still has a grape juice processing plant here. The area has the ideal combination of sunshine, rainfall and soils for grapes and is on the Lake Erie Wine Trail. Westfield is also close enough to Chautauqua and the Institution, which is another reason that people choose to retire in the area. All these factors have combined to create a strong enough community to sustain the WSCR and other charities through economic hardships and vicissitudes.

While I am admittedly a biased observer, Westfield and Chautauqua have a quality of kindness that is so noticeable among WCSR people and cats. This appears in little snippets of local history as well. For example, a book I found in the local library about the towns along Route 20 had a unique chapter on Westfield. Route 20 runs east-west right across northern New York State and other towns' histories centered around special museums, manufacturing pasts, major historic events and current tourist attractions.

The chapter on Westfield was about the Blizzard of '96, a historic storm that dumped over 30 inches of snow in the area. It shut down Interstate 90, the New York State Thruway, which runs just north of Westfield, leaving hundreds of motorists stranded in below-freezing temperatures. In Westfield, the Sheriff gathered a convoy of cars and headed out to the Thruway to guide the stranded motorists back to the town. The people of Westfield opened their houses to the unexpected guests, who found hot meals, comfortable beds and good company instead of a dangerous night in the cold and dark on the highway. They were able to resume their journey safely the next day.

Another historical event marker, which is in fact the most significant piece of public sculpture in Westfield, shows the same qualities of civility and kindness, so necessary and so frequently absent in our world. The Bedell-Lincoln Memorial, located across the street from the village green, immortalizes in bronze the 1861 meeting between President-Elect Abraham Lincoln and 12-year-old Grace Bedell of Westfield. Bedell had written a letter to Lincoln after his election, advising him to grow a beard to give him the gravitas needed for his position and because "all the ladies like whiskers." The meeting took place when the train carrying Lincoln to his Inauguration in Washington stopped at Westfield. Bedell presented him a small bouquet of roses and Lincoln shook her hand and reportedly asked what she thought of his new appearance. As the sculpture records this encounter, Bedell, in pigtails, stands awestruck and dropping flowers from her bouquet, while the great statesman extends a hand in greeting. As a statement of civic identity, this tableau is miles removed from the statues of winged victories and riflemen that decorate village greens elsewhere, however worthy those causes may have been.

These qualities have survived the relentless innovations and disruptions of the twentieth century and the hardships of the twenty-first. They exist not only in history books and public monuments but in everyday life and civility. At WSCR, the bond of kindness extends to the relationship between humans and cats, mysterious, tangible and a sign of hope.

Celeste recalls that she once wrote an article in the WSCR newsletter about the cruelty of abandoning cats. She was inspired by an image she saw a long time ago in a magazine, back in 1968, which has stayed in her mind ever since. That ad for the animal rescue group Nat Cat, the National Cat Protection Society in Orange County, California, showed a tiny, drenched and miserable black kitten, with a piece of cord around its neck. It had been rescued from a deliberate drowning and luckily found a good home. But this image planted the seed of an idea and over the years she followed the work of Nat Cat and other animal welfare groups. She was very much influenced by the writings of Richard Calore, an animal welfare officer who founded Nat Cat.

The Nat Cat shelter would never turn away a homeless cat. For Richard Calore, Nat Cat and the shelter were a way of repaying the kindness of a cat he met in France where he served during World War II. The brave creature shared his foxhole, keeping him warm and providing friendship in a desolate and dangerous place.

Celeste herself originally got involved with animal rescue through the Northern Chautauqua Canine Rescue. In September 1999 her husband, F. Gibbs Kerns, a highly respected attorney, passed away. For a memorial, she named the shelter as one of the organizations to receive donations, at the suggestion of the funeral director. The donations poured in from his wide circle of friends and colleagues.

Celeste was invited to join the Board of Directors of the Canine Rescue and gradually became more and more involved with the dog shelter, visiting to feed and walk the dogs. She and Judy Loomis were close friends, as their husbands had been friends since their schooldays. That was how Judy got her start with animal rescue. "Celeste got me into this," she says. Initially, they volunteered together at the Canine Rescue.

But over time it became clear that there was a need for a similar shelter for cats and the WSCR was born.

Celeste talks about two of the cats that she's fostering right now. One is the adorable CC, short for Cookies and Creme, a tiny black and white kitten who will reach out an endearing paw to visitors of whom she approves. The other is Charlie 2, a herringbone tabby kitten, about six months old, who had an infection in both eyes. With care, he regained some sight in one eye and can see dimly. Part of the other eye had to be removed in surgery. He is expected to recover well from the surgery but will be a special needs cat, needing a home where his disability will not be a problem and he can get the care he needs. Celeste has been fostering him since June, for nearly six months.

She tells me that if she has a specialty, it is caring for cats that have special medical needs or those who need extra care. The cats themselves, she says, are mostly cooperative, perhaps realizing that she's helping them. They have been through hardship and suffering and understand that they are now being looked after and loved. CC and Charlie 2 both found happy forever homes.

In what's known in online cat communities as 'Foster Fail', Celeste decided to adopt little CC and they couldn't be happier. Charlie 2, in spite of having only one eye, has a jaunty presence and was featured on the WSCR Facebook page wearing a stylish French-style beret. He found a happy family and runs around and plays like any other cat. His disability does not hamper him one bit.

There's no doubt in my mind that the little black kitten in that picture picked Celeste, all those years ago, to become a champion for all lost, abused and hurt cats and other creatures. With everything that she and her friends and associates have achieved, Celeste is far from being content to rest on her laurels. Her thoughts are with those cats who are still outside, injured or sick, lonely and afraid. "It's starting to get cold," she said as we left the family restaurant where we met for lunch one bleak November afternoon. By the end of the week, the snow had set in.

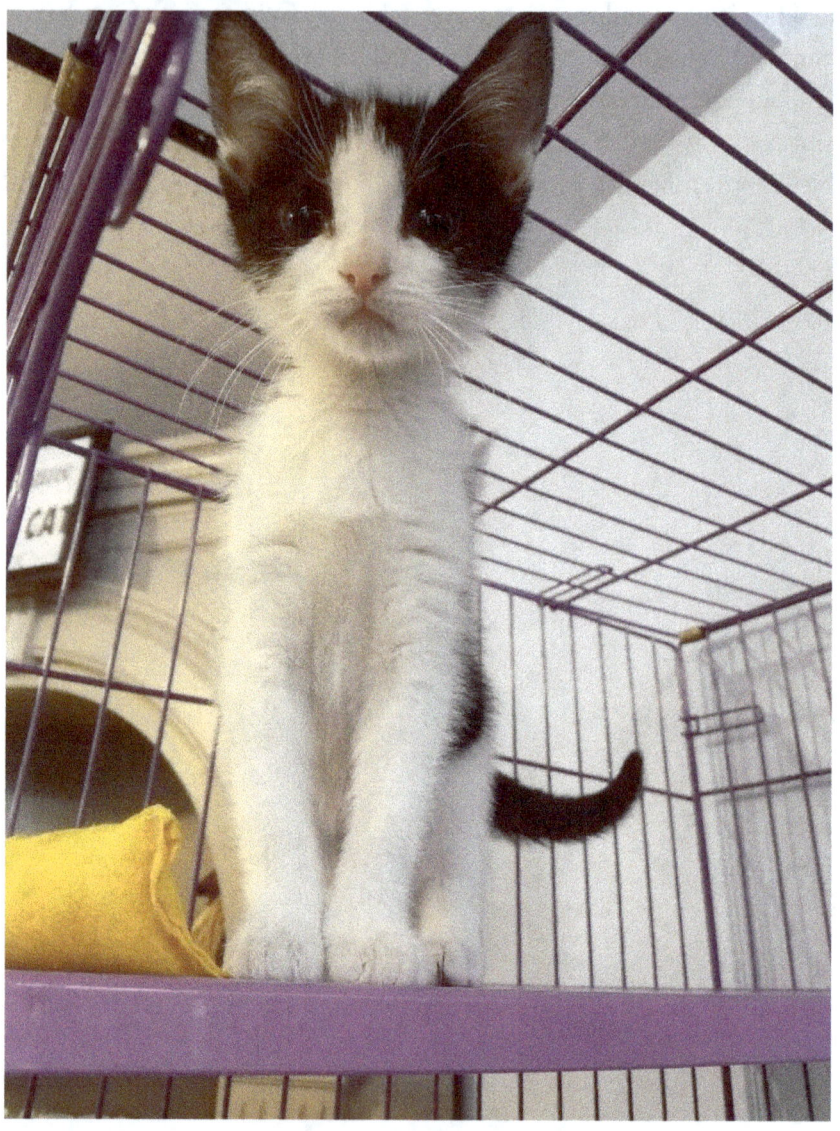

Little CC looking for her forever home. It's a serious matter. December 2016

3

Daring Rescues

Ordinarily, people might do a few animal rescues in their lifetime, and these are branded forever in their memory. The contrast between the beauty and innocence of the animals and their distressing condition can be almost unbearable. Then there's the anxiety not to hurt the animal any further if it is already injured or sick. And sometimes they can be just plain difficult to catch, making the rescue a nerve-wracking process.

WSCR staff find and rescue cats that have been injured, abandoned, or in some other way mistreated every week. Sometimes the cats are so sick or injured that they are glad to be rescued and held. At other times, they are frightened, suspicious and desperate to get away. And a cat that doesn't want to be caught can get up plenty of dodges before finally giving up and allowing itself to be caught.

In the end, as Karen says with her years of experience, it all comes down to one thing: when you've got them, hold on and don't let go. Her method of rescuing cats or kittens is simple, once you've caught them: "the one thing you have to do is that you've got to hold on." Even if you're scratched and bitten, if they fight and squirm and cry, if your emotions are shredded by the cat's distress, you don't let go. And it's necessary to be prepared ahead of time, both emotionally and logistically, because you never know when you'll find a cat that needs to be rescued. Or where you'll have to go to rescue it.

WSCR is entirely staffed by volunteers, with a lot of help from family and friends. For a long time, the rescue squad at WSCR consisted mainly of Karen and her son, Max, who had recently graduated from high school. He had been volunteering at WSCR since he was fifteen. He has a great affinity for the cats and is very good at looking after them. He even knows how to bottle feed kittens, knowing to hold them against the heart, where they feel safe.

A few years ago, he got a call from a school friend, Desiree, who had heard a cat crying inside a ditch next to the railway tracks. She lived nearby and was out for a walk when she heard the cries. The poor cat was trapped among the prickly bushes at the bottom of the ditch and was in a bad way. The thorns made it difficult to reach the cat, but that didn't stop Max. Getting into the ditch full of thorn bushes and out again with a badly injured, fully grown cat was incredibly hard to do, but he managed. He was very young at the time, just about fifteen or sixteen, but didn't hesitate for a moment or consider the risks to himself. The cat was too badly injured to survive. It had been trapped in that place for days and the wounds were infected. It had to be euthanized.

It's difficult enough to reach the cat to be rescued, but sometimes that's only the start of the rescue. The hardest part can be catching them. Cats and even kittens can be very active and they have teeth and claws

36

that they're not shy about using if frightened. The story of the feral cat colony behind the Freeport Restaurant in North East is told in Chapter 8, but it all began with a tiny kitten that Karen saw there, running around a dumpster in the parking lot. He was a scrawny little thing and she just reached out and grabbed him. He didn't want to be caught however and fought and bit. But even with the blood running down her arm, she held on. Her husband told her to let it go, but she tried to explain, all the while being scratched and bitten by a furious wriggling, struggling kitten, that if you let go, you have to catch them again and get bitten again. If you hang on, you do get bitten, but only once.

Happily, the scrawny kitten was adopted by Karen and named Roscoe. He has grown into a large, beautiful orange and white haired cat who is much loved by his humans. Roscoe's sister, Kit, caught a little later, is less friendly to humans and remains suspicious. She too lives with Karen, but in an area of the house set apart for semi-ferals, where they can be safe and warm and live their lives as they prefer, with minimal human interaction.

Another memorable rescue involved crawling under a porch in Chautauqua, on Christmas Eve. That was when Karen had just started volunteering with WSCR. She answered that rescue call with Carol, who volunteers at the Christmas Store. Two kittens had been found in the crawl space under the porch and brought to the police station at the Chautauqua Institution. They called WSCR to take in the kittens and even tried to feed them while waiting for them to be picked up. But the people at the Institution didn't seem to know what kittens eat, despite their population of brilliant thinkers. They did their best and when Karen and Carol arrived to pick up the kittens, they found them in a box along with a little heap of goldfish crackers. Even though they were fish-shaped, the kittens hadn't touched them.

Before heading back to the shelter, the rescuers had to make sure that there were no more kittens left behind under the house. This necessitated a thorough search in the dark, narrow and cold crawl space under the porch. Not the way most people would choose to spend a festive winter evening, but they wanted to make sure there were no more lost kittens hiding there.

The cats from the Chautauqua Institution, which is what Karen calls them, were among her first fosters. And as often happens with first fosters, she ended up adopting them. Annie and Ava, who came to be called Ava Misbehva, are look-alike grey and beige pastel tortoiseshells. They became best of friends with Roscoe, the tiny rescue from near the Freeport Restaurant who scratched and bit when he was caught. They arrived at Karen's house at almost the same time and grew up together. In fact, Roscoe thinks they're his sisters. In a fine expression of cat logic, he is baffled that Karen should think that Kit, who is actually his sister and looks exactly like him, is his sister. And it's perfectly clear to him that even though Annie and Ava look nothing like him, they are his sisters. Annie and Ava like to sleep on top of a tall bookshelf and every now and again will fall off with a loud thump.

The Homeless Eight of Brocton became homeless after their owner passed away. They had lived as indoor-outdoor cats, but the relatives who had inherited the property decided they didn't want to keep them. And so the cats were turfed out of their home by the new owners of the estate. Forced to live outdoors and to fend for themselves, they became rather wild and timid and had to be live trapped. Karen and WSCR were contacted by Judith Kleckner, a cousin of the deceased gentleman, to help rescue them. Judith also feeds the feral cats near a trailer park in Brocton, all sixty or seventy of them and their story is told in Chapter

6. The Brocton Eight were all rescued and found homes, two of them with Karen.

There was Jojo, a small black cat, rather skittish. The last of the Eight to be caught, because he was so cautious, was Jude, a large black and white cat. He had figured out the traps and how to avoid them. In the end, he had to be drop trapped. A drop trap is also a humane trap but needs someone to operate it. So they had to keep watch, hiding nearby and holding on to a string that has to be pulled to close the trap door. They waited a long time for him and even so, almost missed him when he finally entered the trap and started eating. Karen recalls that "We were talking and didn't see him get in the trap. I turned around and saw him and pulled the string just in time to catch him." Now he lives at Karen's home and that will be his home too, for the rest of his life.

Living outdoors and living rough after having been looked after in a loving home, all of the Brocton Eight had health problems. Jude has respiratory problems and is a noisy breather. But that does not affect his quality of life. Karen feels that many of these cats might have been euthanized by a vet or at another shelter, on the grounds that they would not have a good quality of life. 'Quality of life' is often misjudged, she feels and it's perfectly possible for cats who are not in the best of health, or even missing an eye or a leg to live happy lives. Karen says that cats are amazing in terms of how well they can adapt to life, despite injuries and disabilities. She has seen this many times and recalls three kittens that came to WSCR. They were just under a year old. The dominant kitten had only one eye, but it didn't affect his position in the litter. His disability did not put him at a disadvantage.

Cats, unlike people and even children, don't pick on the weak ones. What puts them at a disadvantage is that they are so dependent not only on the changing fortunes but also the whims of the humans who control their lives. Like Frankie Boy and the Homeless Eight from Brocton, they are at risk of losing their homes and even their lives if conditions change. Cats and their welfare are not considered when humans order their affairs, and this may be one of their greatest vulnerabilities.

———

A seasoned animal rescuer, Karen, is always prepared to help an animal or bird in trouble. Wildfowl rescue is not ordinarily on Karen's to-do list, but she found herself obliged to save a bird one day when driving down Route 20 to Ripley. She saw it floundering around some construction cones in the middle of the two-lane highway and couldn't just leave it there and drive on. She turned around and then had to make another U-turn to reach the bird. Route 20 is a state highway with steady traffic, traveling at high speed. It's always tricky driving on a high-speed undivided carriageway and the construction left even less room for maneuver. She stopped her car as close as she could to the bird, put on the flashers and grabbed a sweater she had in the car. With other vehicles whizzing by dangerously close, she ran to the bird and picked it up. She later brought it to a wildlife rescue in Jamestown, where it made a full recovery.

Not all rescues are as dramatic, but all show the same calm underlying determination not to abandon an animal in distress. It's the great achievement at WSCR that everything that's needed for rescue and care is in place. When a new cat or kitten is brought in, everyone knows their parts and things go smoothly to settle the newcomer. With no fuss or bother, cats and kittens are brought to safety because all the pieces of the rescue operation are in place.

I saw one such rescue in July when all WSCR staff had their hands full with the Christmas in July sale, which takes place at the annual Westfield Arts and Crafts Festival on the village green. A call came in from a homeowner in Ripley, who had a fallen barn on her property. She had seen a cat in the debris and was afraid it was injured. Luckily, she was able to catch it and bring it in to the shelter. Karen and Celeste, who were taking turns at the WSCR table, just extended their watch to the shelter at the same time. When the cat was brought in, Celeste was there to check it for injuries (fortunately there were none) and to put it in a separate room with food, water and litter box until Karen could take it home in the evening. New cats are kept separately until they have been checked by a vet and given their shots. Without any interruption to the busy sale and adoption table at the village green, another feline life was saved.

People call on WSCR to come out and rescue cats all the time and even with very limited resources, Karen will never refuse to help. Very often the rescue team was just Karen and Max and their routine which works very efficiently. She says she can't recall a rescue call that she's ever refused. To the question "How do you do it?" Karen's answer is "How do I not?" She says that you weigh what's important and go with what matters. In her world, rescuing an animal in distress is what matters most. As someone who has made a couple of calls to Karen myself, I am deeply grateful for that spirit.

———

Sometimes and perhaps more often than we know, the rescuers are other cats. Neighborhood ferals, taking pity on a pampered pet who finds herself lost and bewildered, see her right, teaching all they know about how to avoid traffic, where humans put out food and where to

41

find shelter. Until the day she is safely and miraculously reunited with her people. That might seem fanciful, but there are a couple of lost cat stories, including my own experience, that bear out that essential truth.

During a phone conversation back in 2017, Karen had told me about a lost cat in Westfield that everyone was looking for - a sheltered, spoiled, indoors-all-her-life, long-haired cat who accidentally escaped from the family car as they made a brief stop near the toll booth on I-90. The busy four-lane highway is a dangerous place for any cat, and especially so for one who has never dealt with traffic. She was also declawed and out wandering somewhere among the grapes. Her family, driving across the country, were frantic with worry. Searching around the highway and vineyards, they also got in touch with WSCR. Karen and other volunteers went out many times to look for the lost cat and set up a few live traps as well. This went on for a couple of months, but the search never lost steam because the family were so active on social media, even though they couldn't stay in the area to continue searching themselves.

A few years later, I got to hear the rest of the story. The family had continued posting alerts regularly on Facebook and called the searchers long distance with all news and leads they received online. And just when it seemed that there was no hope, Karen heard from a garage just outside Westfield, on Route 20, that the cat had been sighted. The people at the garage put out food for the local strays and she had shown up there. Because of the intensive outreach and flyering done by the family as well as Karen and WSCR, they identified her as the missing cat. It was an emotional reunion with her family, with a lot of unanswered questions and some lessons about how lost cats survive.

Somehow this sheltered, pampered indoor cat had made her way across four lanes of busy interstate traffic, survived a journey of several miles across the vineyards, avoiding predators and other dangers, to end up near kindly people who looked out for the strays. Karen is sure that the local feral cats guided her there, imagining them as gruff country characters helping the elegant and clueless indoor cat to find food and safety. Someday this story will make a great picture book for children, with anthropomorphized country cats in plaids, denim overalls and straw hats and the pampered indoors long-haired cat in somewhat tattered pink chiffon: "Hey, cat, you want to know where there's some food? Just follow me!"

I loved this story especially because it parallels my experience when my own Taffy-Cat was lost for about five days. This wasn't out in the country but a temporary apartment in a semi-suburban neighborhood, where she accidentally got out through a torn window screen at ground level. She had been a farm cat years before but lived mostly indoors after that and she certainly knew nothing of the layout of the building and neighborhood. She too knew nothing of traffic and there was plenty of it on the roads.

The best advice I got during those five nightmarish days was to never give up searching because even very sheltered cats can survive in unfamiliar environments. But they need you to keep the faith to help bring them home. Like the searchers in Westfield, I plastered the neighborhood with flyers and walked almost continuously in an expanding circle of blocks around the apartment building. As the flyers quickly began producing results, with calls of accurate sightings nearby, my beat narrowed down to the areas where she had been seen. It seemed that she was trying to find her way back but kept running into obstacles in the built-up environment. She was also spooked by all the people and noise.

As Karen said, sometimes those who rescue cats can be the unlikeliest people and so it was with Taffy's helpers. There was the Chinese student in the building next door, who called with her exact location though she ran off when she saw him. And the cool guy from Texas who turned out to be a cat person. He owned a farm where they took in strays when the shelters ran out of room and talked me through the search. There was the older lady from the former Yugoslavia who lived in one of the houses with big yards. She shared some special bacon from their breakfast when I told her I was hoping to lure Taffy home with food smells.

There were the generous neighbors who allowed me to search their backyards at all hours of day and night. And of course the likely ones, like the editor and faculty wife who lived down the street who also did cat rescues. She had feeding stations in her backyard for the neighborhood ferals and was almost as frantic with worry as I was and as glad when Taffy came home. There was also the neighbor who taught me the prayer to St. Anthony for lost things and it worked for us.

Perhaps the likeliest person was the Dog, though when he did find her he couldn't tell us how to reach her. This was my brother's Saint Bernard who lived across the street and used to visit Taffy, his best friend. When she disappeared, he was puzzled and sad. I had even called tracker dog detectives who specialize in finding lost cats, but they were too far away to make the trip. And then I thought of asking the Dog to track her. He understood at once and in the backyard, put his nose to the ground and followed her scent in a straight line along the fence in the backyard, into the parking lot next door and then to the opening of a long, narrow space between two garages that led to the backyards of the houses on the next street. Only a cat or squirrel could fit through that passage, so I took the Dog round to the next street and with the owners' permission, he began tracking again in their backyards, going unerringly in a straight line with his nose to the ground. He stopped at a free-standing garage next to a tree and wouldn't budge. The doors were locked and there was no way she could have gotten inside, so I just assumed she was in the general vicinity since this also coincided with a couple of other sightings.

This was where I found her a few days later and realized that she had been actually hiding out on top of the garage, using the tree to climb up. The Dog took me to the exact spot, but he never looked up to show where she was. He was thrilled to be reunited with her a few days later and they remained best friends until he passed away a few years later at the age of fourteen.

I'm not sure if he was one of the likely or unlikely helpers, but it was one of the neighborhood ferals who kept Taffy safe when she was lost. I had occasional glimpses of the little grey tabby when I was out searching in the areas where she was sighted. She seemed to be teaching him to hunt, and he was doubtless clueing her in on where to find food, avoiding traffic and showing her hiding places in the huge backyards of the big old houses backing on to the apartment buildings. That's where the Dog led me and it was where I found her when I went out to look for her at 4 am, with cooked shrimp. That's a quiet hour when a lost cat won't be spooked by noise and people, and it was easy to scoop her up and bring her home. I tried for years to tame the little grey tabby, but only ever caught fleeting glimpses of him, fizzing away at high speed when I came too close. But he did go to the feeding stations down the road and there were cold weather shelters as well.

Both lost cat stories have so many lessons for anyone searching for a missing cat, the first one being to never give up. They're out there somewhere and need you to keep looking. Sometimes, new technology can help. Online cat communities, especially at the local level, are slowly discovering their potential in tracking lost and stray cats. All cat lovers understand the pain of searching for a missing pet, as well as the joy of the reunions. Webcams and security cameras can pick up lost and stray cats who only emerge in the late evenings and nights and images can be shared widely on social media. Experienced cat finders and rescuers can likewise share their knowledge and experience. A recent trend that makes searches and rescues more effective is to connect the frantic owners to helpers with humane traps, tracker dogs and even drone cameras.

Then there's also the remarkable evidence of lost cats being befriended by local strays, who help them find food and shelter. The civil and kind behavior of feral and shelter cats, of which we will see many examples in this book, calls into question all the facile nineteenth-century shibboleths about nature red in tooth and claw and the competition for survival. The world of cats and I suspect most of nature, is more Kropotkin than Darwin and cooperation is the norm as well as the key to evolutionary success.

Kropotkin was a Russian near-contemporary of Darwin who ended up in self-imposed exile in England. Although he acquired fame as an anarchist thinker, he was also a naturalist who wrote about mutual aid in animal societies: "In the animal world we have seen that the vast majority of species live in societies and that they find in association the best arms for the struggle for life: understood, of course, in its wide Darwinian sense—not as a struggle for the sheer means of existence, but as a struggle against all natural conditions unfavorable to the species. The animal species, in which individual struggle has been reduced to its narrowest limits and the practice of mutual aid has attained the greatest development, are invariably the most numerous, the most prosperous and the most open to further progress. The mutual protection, which is obtained in this case, the possibility of attaining old age and of accumulating experience, the higher intellectual development and the further growth of sociable habits, secure the maintenance of the species, its extension and its further progressive evolution. The unsociable species, on the contrary, are doomed to decay." The cats haven't read Kropotkin, as far as we know, but they do look out for each other, for their people, dogs, horses and other friends.

A wish for cats and all creatures

4

Life at the Shelter

The official mission of the Westfield Stray Cat Rescue is: "To rescue stray and abandoned cats and kittens and provide shelter, health care and basic necessities until permanent, responsible and loving homes are found for them.

To promote respect and compassion for all creatures through example and education.

To educate the public about the problems of the stray cat overpopulation and possible solutions.

To promote the use of spay and neuter to control pet overpopulation. WE CARE!"

The rescue and shelter grew during the years that Karen served as director since they never refused to take in any homeless, injured, or lost cat. They also expanded the connections to the local community, which came in handy when the shelter ran out of space or when extra funding was needed.

The shelter is limited to 25 cats and the overflow was housed with fosters in the community. Cats with very young kittens were also placed in foster homes and were brought into the shelter and store every week to be socialized to new people and to meet potential adopters. The success in finding fosters and adopters is an indication of the close bond the shelter had with the community. As the shelter grew, so did the ties to the community - fosters, local businesses, generous donors who could be counted on to fund emergency medical needs for rescued cats and kittens.

Banks, libraries, fire stations churches and stores like Tractor Supply opened their doors to the felines to host adoption events. The WSCR Christmas Store has become an annual event, with the support of local businesses. Each year in November, a local business or property owner donates the use of an empty store space in downtown Westfield to the Thrifty Kitty for the Christmas Store. For two months, WSCR turns the space into a holiday shoppers' paradise, with Christmas and cat-themed items - gifts, housewares, decorations, lights and other delightful finds at bargain prices.

Art galleries, farmers markets and libraries also helped out with various fundraising and adoption events. Much of this cooperation between the shelter and the community is a reflection of the qualities of trust and openness that are part of life in Chautauqua County. The town of Westfield, with its picture-perfect Main Street, village green and traditions of volunteerism has been a good home for WSCR from the very beginning. The cat rescue was founded in 2007 by three friends, Judy Loomis, Celeste Kerns and Hilda Span. At that time they didn't even have a space for a shelter to house the strays and the rescued cats lived in foster homes. WSCR provided medical care for the rescues and found them forever homes. A significant date that remains in her mind,

Celeste says, was February 19, 2007, when they decided to create a cat rescue organization. They sent out letters to people in the community, seeking support and the generous responses they received provided the first funding for setting up WSCR.

Celeste and Judy recalled drawing up plans for the shelter sitting around the kitchen table, in a time-honored fashion. The Board of Directors was created, as required by the incorporation process and the first members were the three original founders. They took turns in answering calls about adoptions, sharing a single cell phone that was passed around between them, depending on whose turn it was to answer phones that day. They used Judy's phone, and the number was widely publicized so people could contact them. She still gets calls to that number, even though she retired a few years ago.

In the early years, when there wasn't a shelter building and the rescues were homed with fosters, it wasn't easy to show the cats to potential adopters. To get the word out about adoptions, they relied on tables at events and flyers posted around town. One of the locations that hosted the adoptions in the early days was Tasty Acres, a family restaurant near the Chautauqua Institution that was an institution in itself. The adoption tables were also sites for fundraising and hosted Bijou's Boutique, with a small selection of crafts and jewelry. Named after a cat at the shelter, the Boutique debuted the catnip pillows made by Judy Loomis. These have become a WSCR hallmark. Judy must have made thousands over the years. She recently completed a batch of three hundred and thinks it may be the last one she'll do. The cats love them since they add a touch of feline comfort and fun to any surroundings.

Institutional landmarks for WSCR were: becoming registered as a nonprofit, buying the building on West Main Street to serve as the shelter and opening the Thrifty Kitty store which became a reliable source of income. When it came to finding a building for the store and shelter, they didn't have much choice in terms of location and layout. They had to go with what was available and affordable. This happened to be the building that used to be the Village Veterinary Clinic, owned by Dr. Robert Rogers. The building became available when the vet clinic moved to its current location next to the fire station, just off Main Street. Dr. Rogers provided medical care for the WSCR rescues until he retired recently. When the veterinary clinic moved, WSCR bought the two-story building and changed it around to suit their needs. The vet's office had used the downstairs area for the clinic and the top floor for the kennels and surgery. The Thrifty Kitty now occupies the first floor, and the cat shelter is upstairs. The entire space has a cheerful, homelike feeling, due to the layout, furniture, decor and most of all, the inhabitants of the building, human and feline. The shelter and The Thrifty Kitty together add a cheerful grace note to Westfield's picture-perfect Main Street.

Funding was scarce in the early years and Judy used her tax refunds to pay for the spay and neuter costs for rescued cats. Once people found out about the existence of the rescue, they began to get cats. A lot of cats, Judy recalls wryly. And it hasn't stopped since. The Thrifty Kitty store opened its doors in the downstairs space in 2011 and the earnings from the store enabled WSCR to buy the building. The shelter upstairs has to meet strict requirements under village zoning regulations, limiting the number of cats, their level of freedom and so on. At present, the shelter is limited to twenty-five cats and another sixty are cared for in foster homes. Foster homes are essential to keeping cats and kittens housed and fed until they find forever homes, because of the space limitations at the shelter.

Being Director of the shelter is a very hands-on job and can take well over forty hours a week. Karen and Priscilla Marsh were at that time co-directors and Celeste appreciated all their hard work, telling me that she couldn't say enough good things about the amount of time they put in, being there for the cats, cleaning, doing the laundry and helping to socialize the cats. It helps the cats in the shelter just to hear human voices and to know that they are not alone. Volunteers and their families put in a lot of hours to make sure the shelter runs smoothly. Karen's family, her husband and son, do a lot at the shelter and even more at home, looking after homeless, sick and injured cats.

Talking with Karen, Celeste and Judy, I see a different side to their work, not apparent to a casual visitor to the shelter or the thrift store. They don't ever give up, taking on the most difficult cases, the injured, disabled and sick, where even the vet would see no hope and recommend euthanasia. Because each cat and kitten, no matter how desperate the situation, has the spark of life and courage. Recognizing this in each Cat and kitten, they are willing to help them fight for their lives. Very often, they succeed.

The shelter itself has a very cheerful and homely feel and the cats are loved and contented. The calm and loving temperament of the cats is one of the first things visitors notice and people who adopt from WSCR cherish this special quality of the shelter's cats. Karen feels that this is very much due to the volunteers, who will make sure that especially shy or timid cats get extra attention and love. Volunteers and staff will often stop by just to say hello to the cats and kittens during the day. Or they will stay after their shifts to make sure that cats get the cuddles and play they need to fulfill their natures.

Upstairs, the shelter has separate areas for different age groups, with kitten, teen and adult rooms. The youngest kittens, and mother cats with kittens, actually live in foster homes until the kittens are old enough to live at the shelter. The rooms are set up as friendly play and living areas, with plenty of toys, room to run around, things to climb and individual cat condos to retreat for quiet time and naps.

Teenage cats are defined as the age group between six months to one and a half years and they are a lively lot. Adult cats tend to be quieter, so it makes sense to give them their own space. Teens are developing their own personalities, moving on from their babyish kittenhood to their adult selves.

Over time, the rooms have been changed and improved as the funds became available. The big front room became the adult cats' room a few years ago. The proceeds from sales at the first, highly successful Christmas Store provided the funding to change the flooring from carpeting to vinyl, which is easier to keep clean. The rooms all have comfortable captain's chairs for visitors to sit and meet the cats. Most of the cats love to cuddle and know exactly what laps are for. Others are content to watch from a benign distance, play with their toys or climb the very sturdy cat trees, or watch the birds outside in the daytime.

Downstairs at the Thrifty Kitty store, visiting cats and kittens can sometimes be found in the large cat condo. They have been brought in by their fosters to be socialized and meet potential adopters. The cat condo in the store is also sometimes used to accommodate cats who aren't getting along too well with others in the rooms upstairs. One such cat was Naomi, a tabby, who was brought in with her two kittens. While the two little tabby rascals were getting up to all kinds of mischief in the teens' room upstairs and enjoying the attention they

54

received on outings to the farmers market, Naomi lived in the store condo and made friends with visitors. When she contracted a urinary tract infection, Tami, Denise, Jessica and other volunteers who worked in the store pitched in to take care of her, remembering her medications no matter how busy it got. She made a good recovery and is heading for her new home, where she will be able to run around and play to her heart's content.

Celeste says that in the evenings, after the rooms and condos have been cleaned and the water changed, the cats are happy to go back into their condos and settle down for the night. Of course, being cats, they will sometimes take over each other's condos or eat each other's food. But it's all good fun and the rooms are calm and restful places. In the daytime, the cats run around and play, but in the evenings they're glad to have a place of their own to retreat to. It's quite funny to watch, she says, as they zoom into their condos as soon as volunteers finish cleaning each one on the evening shift.

Considering the problems that cat owners face in introducing new pets to their homes, I wondered if the shelter had a special process for this. But it hasn't been necessary, because the cats are used to seeing each other come and go. There are no fights or territorial issues. Also, Karen says, cats are not like people and will not pick on new or weak individuals, unlike kids in school. They understand when an animal is in need and will not hurt it. There's a civility among the cats in the shelter, which many observers have also noticed in feral cat colonies. This is quite a necessary corrective to the Hobbesian view which some people hold of animals and the natural world. For cats, at least, a state of strife is not their natural condition. Nor are cats just indifferent to each other. They have a range of behaviors, from polite civility to playfulness to sympathy for each other when it's needed.

The rooms, the kitchen and the office itself are very comfortable, clean places with a friendly feeling. A lot of the furniture - the large office desk shared with Fallon and Buster, the office chair with its leather now marked with scratches, the comfortable wooden captain's chairs in the rooms - comes from Celeste's husband's office.

In the summer of 2015, the Adult Room and Teen Rooms had makeovers, with new cat-friendly shelves attached to the wall. A new vertical climbing area was designed and built by volunteers. Besides climbing, birdwatching is a favorite pastime in the adult cats' room. The large windows look out onto a bird feeder and next to it are giant cat trees with multiple seats and perches for comfortable viewing. It's one of the most popular corners of the room.

When they first come in, cats have to be kept apart until they can be tested for feline leukemia and feline AIDS. Cats who are to be kept separate may be put in the bathroom for short periods, but for a longer time, they go to foster homes. Many fosters have specialties - Celeste and Karen look after cats who are sick or need special care. Celeste also fosters mother cats with nursing kittens, as does Rhoda Graham. The office is used for cats who need to be kept separate from the others for some reason, though for medical isolation they would go to a foster home. At present, Fallon has an office mate, a sleek, rather shy black cat called Buster. He has to be in a separate space from the other adult cats because he is on a special diet and the other cats are not supposed to eat his food. He's not supposed to eat their food either but manages to sneak into Fallon's condo and eat her food.

One of the first things to do when a new cat comes in is to give it a name. The naming of cats, as T.S. Eliot said, is a serious thing. Naming cats is also a practical necessity, so that proper records can be kept, and their medical records can be tracked. With so many cats, there's always a need for names and shelter staff have some resources to draw upon. There's a book of baby names in the office and a list of names that were collected through a competition for kids. Visitors to the store and shelter, people who bring in the cats, vet techs, volunteers and others are always being asked for names for the cats. Judy has named hundreds of cats in her time, using names from her family, shelter staff, TV shows and celebrities. The names are sometimes changed when the cats and kittens go to their foster homes or forever homes. That's when it becomes easier to see aspects of their personalities that suggest suitable names.

There's a special naming convention for mother cats with kittens and the kittens are given names beginning with the same initial as the mother. For example, a mother cat rescued from the tavern in Ripley where Fallon lived, had four kittens. Giving them all names starting with the letter 'T' - Tessa, Tizzy, Tootsie and Tintin - made it easier to identify them as litter-mates. They were eventually adopted in pairs. Sometimes cats are named for the holidays or the season they are brought in. A cat who was brought in around St. Patrick's Day was named Shamrock and her kittens also had Irish names.

————

Most people who decide to adopt a cat choose a kitten, because of their cuteness and charm. This sometimes leads to older cats being overlooked. But teenage and adult cats are actually easier to adopt because their personalities are known. Do they like to snuggle, are they playful and good with kids and other pets? These qualities matter when choosing a new pet for your home. The WSCR cat adoption form also asks the kind of questions that people should ask themselves before adopting a pet. Do they have children or other pets? Do they own their homes or rent and if they rent, do they have permission in writing from the landlord to keep a cat? Do they have any experience with cats? WSCR asks for a couple of personal references and a veterinarian reference if there are already pets in the house and these are followed up carefully.

Anyone adopting a cat is making a lifelong commitment, for anywhere from ten to fifteen to twenty years. To protect the cats, adopters undertake to follow these terms:

1. I will house the cat in my home as a companion. I will not sell, abandon, or give it away.
2. I will provide proper and sufficient housing, food, water and exercise, as well as kind treatment at all times.
3. I will have the cat vaccinated on schedule and provide proper and appropriate veterinary treatment at my own expense.
4. I will not permit the cat to run at large or become a public nuisance.
5. If for any reason I can no longer keep the cat, I will contact Westfield Stray Cat Rescue and relinquish ownership to them.

If, someday, we progress to the point of having a bill of rights for cats, it might look something like this.

In fact, I've come to feel that a world that works for cats would also be one that works for humans. The distressing opposite of adoptions is when a cat or dog has to be surrendered by an owner who can no longer afford to care for pets. As of 2023, with rising economic distress, shelters around the country are seeing an increase in surrenders. Social media and especially Facebook groups reveal some of the stories of desperation behind the appeals for new homes. People who work but can no longer afford a place to live or have trouble making ends meet have to make the heart-wrenching decision to part with their companions. For an observer, the logical solution to these grief-stricken exchanges would be to ensure that people did not have to leave their homes and were able to feed themselves and their families and pets. This might seem almost too simple, but one can almost hear the cats saying, that's why it would work.

Photos of cats ready for adoption

5

The Habitat

Rescuing cats and kittens is hard enough in and of itself, but then there are the difficult ones. These are the ferals, the cats with special needs, the older ones for whom it is harder to find forever homes, or those who are too sick or badly injured to be adopted. I discovered early on that Karen has a special place in her heart for them. Even if a cat or kitten is missing a limb or has lost an eye, or if it has a chronic disease which makes it difficult to adopt, she sees that it still has the will to live and will do everything she can to help it survive and thrive. She even has a special place in her home for them.

This is Karma's Hope, a habitat for feral and special needs cats completed in July 2016, as a refuge for kitties who can't find anywhere else to live. The Habitat, located on the grounds of Karen's home, is named for a charismatic little kitten called Karma Hope. Karma came to WSCR as a tiny kitten, with her back legs paralyzed. She was so small when she was brought in that she had to be fed from a bottle. The vet actually thought that she wouldn't survive and suggested that she should be euthanized. But she was so spirited and so full of life, that Karen thought she deserved a chance.

She couldn't stay at the shelter, so she went to Karen's home. "She was the funniest, spunkiest little cat," Karen says. Karma lived for three happy years in Karen's home with the other animals, fifteen cats and three dogs. She quickly made a place for herself in the house and in everyone's hearts. Her disability was not a handicap. At Karen's house, all floors are wood or tile, which are easier to keep clean than carpeting, with so many animals. As all households with both dogs and cats discover, the best feeding arrangement is to keep dog food bowls on the floor and cat bowls on a table, to keep the dogs from eating the cats' food as well. Karma's food had to be kept on the floor so she could reach it, but none of the other animals, cats or dogs, would bother her while she was eating.

As Karen talks about Karma, it's easy to see the deep bond that existed between them and how the little cat had completely won her over. Recognizing her will to live and her lively interest in everything around her, Karen was caught up in her spirit. Life couldn't have been easy for either of them, but what Karen recalls is her fun-loving and mischievous personality. Karma wore a diaper since she couldn't control her bodily functions. Even so, she has to be given a bath each day. The daily bath was the part she hated, and she would run and hide behind the sofa, peeking out from behind like a cartoon cat. She managed to get around at quite a pace, wearing tiny socks on her back paws.

WSCR is always looking for people to adopt special needs cats and they did find someone who wanted to adopt Karma. But even though it would have been a good home, Karen found that when the time came, she couldn't give her up. So Karma lived for three happy, loving years in Karen's house and passed away in the spring of 2016. In her memory, Karma's Hope Habitat for special needs and difficult to place cats was opened in the summer. There are now nine cats at the Habitat and one more will move in soon.

With donated materials, labor and time, construction began in July 2016 and by fall, ten shelters were ready for their occupants. The ten-by-thirty-foot Habitat is built at the back of Karen's home, which is a large farmhouse in Ripley. Officially described as a lifetime haven for special needs and hard to place felines, Karma's Hope is a group home environment with both indoor shelter and outdoor access for the cats. The outdoor space is enclosed with a high chain link fence that keeps the cats safe and stops them from straying. The enclosed space has a roof and feral cat shelters, built by volunteers. In the winter, there is a heated indoor space for the cats.

The cat shelters are little chalet- style wooden homes, with sloping roofs, insulation and two entrances/exits for safety. Denise Spencer, who is also the Treasurer and Record Keeper for WSCR, found directions for building feral cat shelters online. A group of volunteers that included Denise's father and his friends from church and Rhoda Graham's husband and his friends used the designs to build the sturdy little homes.

The cats at the Habitat are the ones that are difficult to adopt and that's why they get extra love and attention from Karen. In most cases, they have been at WSCR for a year or longer without being adopted. There's Remi and his sister, who were found in the woods. There's Pepper, who sprays and Elsie, who is semi-feral. There's the unfortunately-but-all-too-accurately-named Stinky and of course, there's a story. Her real name is Margot and she's a lovely long-haired grey with brilliant green eyes and a loving temperament. She was adopted out a couple of times, but each time came back to the shelter. She would go out on very good terms with her new family and do very well in the beginning. But each time, after a few days, she would stop using her litter box and instead poop in the most unsuitable places, including beds. Naturally, she came back to the shelter each time. Karen's husband called her the 'cash cow', because the adoption fee paid each time is not refundable and suggested, not quite seriously, that the shelter should continue sending her out to earn more money. However, WSCR decided that it was too wearing on both the cat and her adoptive families and so she came to live at the Habitat.

Kiki, who is a tortoiseshell, had been at the shelter for a few years. As an older cat, it was harder for her to be adopted. At the shelter, she had started to become more withdrawn and would stay inside her cat condo even during the day, when the doors are open to let the cars roam around the room. The moment she walked into the Habitat, she just changed completely. Karen feels it may have been that the outdoors were much closer, so she could hear the birds, chipmunks and other creatures. Even after dark, the Habitat is never completely silent and she may have found it comforting, compared to the silence at the shelter every evening after the volunteers leave to go to their homes.

Scotty is a black cat whose tail had to be amputated because of an injury. He also had a birth defect that gave him a strange marking around the eyes. Overall, his appearance made it harder to find him a home. Like Elsie, he felt at home as soon as he came to the Habitat from the shelter, and he loves his life there. The tenth cat for the Habitat is currently in a holding zone at the shelter. Like all new cats, he has to be vaccinated, neutered, dewormed and defleaed before being released with the other cats. With so many cats in close quarters, it's important to be sure that they're all healthy.

For all of these cats, Karma's Hope has become the ideal lifetime home, where they can lead happy, safe and fulfilling lives. Recently a little tiger kitten was brought into the shelter, also with her back legs paralyzed like Karma. The volunteer who looked after her named her Hope, without knowing that it was Karma's name as well. When the vet told Karen about the kitten's condition, she said, we can work with it. He was surprised because, in such situations, most vets recommend euthanasia. But Karen is determined to give them a life and Karma showed it could be a full and happy one. Hope lives at Karen's house as a long-term foster and probably will stay there for the rest of her life.

The cats who have problems getting adopted or even just surviving are Karen's special projects. They have a will to live and she will do everything can to support them. As we talked, I began to see that it is the cats that need special care, that are difficult to place, that are still out there living dangerous, lonely lives, that occupy her thoughts. Having seen about a thousand cats come and go, her thoughts are still about those who need help and what she can do about it.

————

Even after retiring from her position as director at WSCR, Karen continues to have a house full of cats who would be difficult to rehome anywhere else. They're all characters and well loved and the truth is that she wouldn't part with them even if there were other homes for them. This makes the household very cat-oriented, though there are three dogs as well who hold their own among all the feline goings-on.

Cats can be helpers and healers too and Karen's cats have been a help to her instead of a burden through her illness. There's Chatterbox, a classic grey tabby who has taken the role of bodyguard and protector to Karen as she deals with chronic health problems. There's a whole scrum of greys, tabbies, gingers and blacks who live together peacefully, sharing meals on the dining table and space on their special couch. There are separate areas in the house for cats that prefer to avoid human company, where they can live their lives as they like best.

With all her love for animals, especially cats and the experience she has of rescue, Karen would be a great educator and advocate for them. Her work in TNR and in running a shelter that feels more like a home than a prison for the animals, surely has a wider message for policymakers and educators about how we want to treat the animals with whom we share the earth and our lives. Karen's work embodies long-term trends in how strays and shelter animals are to be treated. It shows how to end the "euthanization" of millions of stray, lost and feral dogs and cats in shelters every year, with TNR as the humane and more effective way of tackling the problem of pet overpopulation. By providing a home for cats who may be in less than perfect physical condition, who may be euthanized elsewhere, she shows how the definition of "quality of life" must be expanded to give them a chance at living their best possible lives. And her infectious spirit of love for all animals and determination not to let them down is a model for a more ethical future where cats and other animals are treated as persons rather than property.

Perhaps most important and necessary, charismatic and articulate advocates for cats and other stray animals like Karen can help remove the censure and stigma that often meets efforts to rescue and help creatures in misfortune. Anyone who has ever tried to help an animal in distress has likely also faced discouragement and callousness from various people including family members, neighbors and friends who would rather not take the trouble. These strictures against rescuing animals are surprisingly uniform across cultures - the unfortunate creatures are "dirty," they may be carrying diseases (almost never, actually), they cost too much to feed, they're too much trouble to look after. The cumulative effect is to stifle the instincts of altruism and care and to surround their practice with anxiety and social stigma.

The discouragement can also take institutionalized forms, with local authorities cracking down on feral community caretakers and even refusing permission to TNR. Some state park authorities too prohibit feeding feral cats on the grounds that they are wild animals, depriving them of crucial support in difficult environments. And unfortunately, environmentalists sometimes position themselves in hostility to feral cats, based on faulty models widely publicized by established institutions like the Audubon Society and the Smithsonian. This makes cats a convenient scapegoat for the environmental destruction caused by humans. In Australia and California, cruel "culling" programs of stray felines have been implemented, even though these have been proven to be ineffective, while rejecting the option to TNR, which actually works to reduce feral populations.

As a result, animal helpers and especially feline rescuers perforce tend to be publicity-shy and don't have much of a platform to discuss their work, even among themselves. Which is a great pity, since their work arises from all that is best in human nature. Altruism may be "impractical," which is why so many shelters and rescuers suffer from burnout due to lack of support and recognition, but it is an educational necessity that will help determine the shape of our collective future. While laws against animal cruelty, discussed in Chapter 8, can only take us so far, education is the key to freeing us to follow our best instincts and to creating social priorities aligned with them. Once again, we are back to the question of sovereignty and whether our individual and collective efforts should be directed towards kindness and justice, or power based on fear and cruelty. It does indeed begin with the cats.

Karma kitten supervising the laundry

THE HABITAT

6

The Thrifty Kitty

The Thrifty Kitty is a cheerful, bright place that draws people in. The connection to the shelter and the presence of the cats is an added attraction that makes it difficult to pass by. The presence of cats and kittens in the store adds a special appeal. There's a large cat condo in the front room and it usually has one or two cats or kittens visiting. These are cats in foster care who need forever homes. They come to the store one day a week, to be socialized, to meet people and possibly be adopted. The visiting cat condo is right next to a special shelf with gifts for pets and pet lovers. The gifts include catnip toys made by Judy Loomis from quilting squares, blankets, dishes and even Hello Kitty pajamas for kids. Inevitably, there are also cat-themed collectibles and cat books. There's cat-themed artwork on the walls and behind the checkout counter, a picture wall of cats and kittens who are ready for adoption. Visitors can go upstairs to the shelter to meet the adoptable cats and kittens.

Then there's the great location, right on Main Street, just across the street from the village green with its spreading trees and church steeple, restaurants and art galleries. Opening the store was a big step for WSCR, both in terms of the effort required and by stepping up outreach to the community. Judy Loomis was inspired to borrow the idea of a thrift store to support the cat rescue from the Chautauqua County Humane Society in Jamestown. Their thrift store, Second Chances, has been a reliable source of income for the shelter and other programs.

The store is staffed entirely by volunteers, many of whom put in thirty to forty hours a week. No one, including the manager, Art Kinney, or volunteers like Tami and Ramona Rosado who give the store thirty hours a week each, gets any pay. Except, as Karen says, the joy of what they do. Art Kinney, the store manager, puts in five full days a week, volunteering his time and experience in retail. He retired a few years ago, after working for thirty-five years at Carnahan's Menswear in Jamestown. He loves retail and the volunteerism, the people and of course, the cats.

No two days are alike, he says, but he's a people person and can handle it. The store is a center for the community, and he's made many friends here. One such family are actually his neighbors. They live down the street from him, but he met them at the store and is now "Mr. Art" to the kids. Like other WSCR volunteers, Art is very connected to the community and is in charge of the Ripley chapter of The Grange.

The store, like the shelter, is a labor of love for the volunteers. Judy recalls that when they first opened, she didn't want the store to look like a typical dreary second hand store. She and Celeste were aiming for a boutique look when they set it up and the volunteers continue this tradition. Volunteers include retirees as well as people working full time, who devote their days off to the kitties. Their efforts have produced a shopping environment with the look and feel of a comfortable, well-kept home, possibly in the country, where you can browse for a pleasant hour for fun, cheerful and practical things.

The store is full of housewares, linens and kitchenware, many with a very appealing vintage look. Bowls, mugs, placemats, sheets, lamps, clothing, shoes - even if you didn't actually need any, you may end up getting some and then figuring out a use for them later. It's a great place for bargains, especially for good clothing for very low prices, which makes it popular for families and back-to-school shopping. And also for stocking up on winter necessities like boots, hats, scarves and gloves. Books, music and handbags round out the essentials of life.

The general consensus is that people leave happy, with their arms full of bargains and intending to come back. The store is a big success and ensures a steady income for the shelter. It is a much more reliable source of income than donations, which can vary a great deal. Initially, it took some time for the store to really take off and they received donations only about once a week. Now there are donations coming in every day and people know to come here for great bargains. There are also vintage and antique items which are valuable. Some of these are sold online on the eBay store. Sande Dotson, also volunteering her time and talent, manages the WSCR online eBay store.

The store is a financial anchor for the shelter, and it has also become a focal point for the community. Often people will come in looking for household goods and decor at bargain prices to furnish new homes and kitchens. Art is very sympathetic to those who are on a budget. He will help out people who are just starting out or starting over by just handing them a couple of large bags to go around the store and pick out anything they like, on the house. Sometimes, families that have been burnt out of their homes and have lost everything will come to the store to furnish their new homes. Art will likewise give them a free day's shopping. He's been burnt out of his home once, he says, and he knows what that's like.

The store and shelter become a place that people rely on, even for matters that don't concern cats. Karen recalls a young girl who was a frequent visitor to the store. There was the day when her stepmother called for help because she was concerned that the girl hadn't been well and might not have money for food. She couldn't be there herself and asked if someone at the store could look up the daughter and make sure she was all right. Judy Loomis did so, and took her grocery shopping, spending her own money to make sure she had all she needed. It was a mission that had nothing to do with the shelter or feline rescue, but the lady who called felt that she could trust the people at WSCR to care for her daughter when she couldn't be there herself. She reimbursed Judy later for the groceries.

Celeste has been involved with the Thrifty Kitty since the beginning. Before the store opened, she recalls that WSCR used to run yard sales with donated items at different locations, including Eason Hall in Westfield. There were two major sales a year. The yard sales were a lot of work and they were very much at the mercy of the elements. If it rained, all paper and fabric items would be ruined before they could be moved to safety. Setting up the thrift store was a big step, but it also made sales more convenient, eliminating the need to rent venues for the yard sales and storage for unsold items.

The can-do spirit that tackles challenges with cheerfulness, faith and hope is the WSCR hallmark. When the store first opened, all they had was some very old, rusty, dilapidated metal shelving, "practically scrap metal," from a store that had closed. Judy recalls dressing these up in fabric and ribbons to hide their dreadfulness. The tradition of cheerfully making do with whatever was at hand has continued through the work of shelter even with a change of guard.

Celeste says that she is constantly amazed at the kinds of people and efforts the store inspires. Over the years, more and more volunteers have signed up. Westfield is a close- knit, fairly thriving community with a strong tradition of volunteerism. Many WSCR volunteers are also active in the local food bank, the hospital auxiliary and other charities. The inhabitants are mostly blue-collar families, who work hard for what they have. Merchants along Main Street do struggle, due to competition from online and big box stores. But they are always willing to contribute prizes for raffles and to support WSCR in other ways. Fundraising efforts always find a good response. It is a generous community.

The Thrifty Kitty windows are a work of art in themselves and are changed every month or so. Karen does the windows and decides on each month's theme along with Art. Sometimes the windows are seasonal, and others refer to local history and culture. A donation of Amish decorations inspired a "Sampler of Local History & Culture." A sign that Karen found, "Bring your own sunshine," became the centerpiece for a summer-holiday display with beach bags, books and other essentials for a day by the water. However, a summer display of a model Harley Davidson with a stuffed toy pig astride, captioned "Just me and my hog" met with disfavor from Naomi, the tabby with two young kittens. She lived in the cat condo in the store while waiting to go to her forever home and was allowed to run around in the evenings after the store closed. One day, she chose to knock over the pig and rip up the flowers. This when she was very careful with all the glassware and knickknacks temptingly arrayed on open shelves. Many a cat would have spent a happy hour knocking those off the shelves one by one, but not Naomi. The pig display was the only one she ever destroyed. Tami had a theory about this: "Maybe she just doesn't like pigs."

Christmas is a special time at the Thrifty Kitty. The store is decorated and there's also a special Christmas Store at a nearby location. Judy Loomis has been in charge of setting up the Christmas Store from the beginning and it has also become a meeting point for the community in many different ways. The location varies each year and is a temporary space on or near Main Street, donated each year by different owners. WSCR does not have to pay rent for the space and only picks up the tab for the utilities. Donations for the store begin coming in each year directly after Christmas, as people take down their decorations, so by November there's enough to stock an entire store dedicated to the holidays.

There are special Christmas items for sale, of course. Decorations, tree ornaments, mugs, dinnerware, linens, stuffed toys, small gifts, stockings, stocking stuffers and other items are all in excellent condition, just asking to be picked and taken to your own home. There's a special Christmas tree with ornaments and each ornament has an item written on it. Visitors are asked to pick one and bring back the item named for the shelter. These items include basic supplies like paper towels, cleaning supplies, blankets, towels and of course, toys for the cats. Once the store closes after Christmas, WSCR donates the unsold things to other charities. Some are saved for the Christmas in July sale at the Arts and Crafts Festival in Westfield.

For days and even weeks, I badgered WSCR staff and volunteers with questions about the store, trying to place its special quality. It's in the love all of them have for the work they do and for the reason behind the work. It's in the love of the community for the shelter, expressed through regular donations of all kinds of useful, fun and intriguing things. It's in the way that the merchandise is arranged, with a real feeling for creating an environment that combines a homely atmosphere with the lure of thrift shopping. And then, I realized, it's also the cats, the genii loci of the place. They won't ever come out and tell you directly, but the cheerfulness of the store and the shelter, I realized, was the cats' indirect answer to my question: what do the kitties think of WSCR?

Summer decorations at the Thrifty Kitty

7

Flipping the Semi-ferals

The sheer number of homeless and feral cats is staggering. There are five times more homeless cats than homeless people in the US. Life isn't easy for them. Even though feral cats have adapted to living wild, they have a very short life expectancy. Living alone in the wild, they suffer from cold, hunger and sickness. In recent years, Karen and other volunteers have teamed up with people in the area who have been feeding and caring for feral cats and with the Chautauqua County Humane Society, for a Trap Neuter Return or TNR program. As more and more such projects get underway across the country and feline advocates share their experiences over the Internet, TNR is emerging as the best way to handle the problems of homeless cats and feral cat overpopulation.

As feline advocates have discovered, TNR is a highly effective way of reducing the feral population. Over 7 years, a single pair of cats and their offspring can hypothetically produce a total of 402,000 new cats, many of whom will be homeless. While real life does not follow mathematical formulae, the problem of feline homelessness is still immense. Reducing the number of kittens born in the wild is the best way of reducing the population of homeless cats. Statistics from around the country show that in areas with active TNR programs, shelter intakes for cats drop dramatically. The experience of feline advocates in Chautauqua County bears this out. With active TNR programs that WSCR carried out with help from the Chautauqua County Humane Society, there was a drop in shelter intakes. However, for a couple of years after Karen's retirement, WSCR stopped TNR in Westfield and consequently saw a huge jump in the number of homeless kittens. As the shelter and fosters struggled to home them all, the need to restart TNR became clear.

Some feline advocates oppose TNR because they feel it's not safe to release the cats back into the wild. This is an issue that has divided cat advocates, even though the cats being released are going back to their familiar territory. WSCR will only undertake TNR in settings when there is someone who will continue to feed the ferals and watch out for them after they are released. In many cases, feral cat shelters and cat houses have been set up by their caretakers. Kittens are never released back into the wild since they can be socialized and adopted. With older cats, Karen and other TNR advocates will try and 'flip' them into becoming tame so they can be adopted. There's a high chance of success and most feral cats can be flipped, though it takes time and patience. Karen actually calls them the semi-ferals, which is a more accurate description, since all cats can become accustomed to some level of interaction with humans. Flipping essentially involves getting the cats accustomed to humans, so they can live indoors comfortably. If there's any chance that a cat can be flipped, tamed and adopted, it will not be released back.

Feral colonies can range in size from sixty or seventy cats to just a few individuals. Typically, they come to the attention of WSCR when a colony caretaker, who has been feeding the cats, asks for help. For the past three years, Karen has been carrying out TNR in Brocton, with help from Judith Kleckner, who has been feeding sixty to seventy feral cats there for a couple of years. Rhoda Graham, a volunteer who is also the official WSCR photographer and fosters cats and kittens, helped with the TNR operation in Brocton. Pam Rosotto from Fredonia, whose pet project is TNR, was also part of the Brocton project.

TNR goes on continuously through the summer. Humane traps are used and WSCR never leaves them unattended because there's a chance that the cats will hurt themselves struggling when they are first caught. If someone is there to watch when the cat is trapped, a towel or blanket can be thrown over the trap and that usually calms then down. Three cats are trapped at a time and taken to the Chautauqua County Humane Society in Jamestown, where they are fixed, vaccinated and provided medical care if needed. They are released back after one week. The same day, three more cats are trapped, and the cycle begins again, continuing all summer long. It takes a major effort and many bites and scratches, but the results are worth it. This year, there were no homeless kittens in Brocton. TNR is funded by donations from groups like the American Legion.

Adult ferals are only released back if they can't be flipped and remain hostile or terrified of humans. Since WSCR only does TNR in locations where there is a caretaker who will continue to feed the cats and look out for them, when they are released it is back to their familiar surroundings. And the cats are happy to go back home. Karen says the moment the carrier doors are opened, they're off like a shot and vanish into their familiar habitat. They're coming back home and settle in very quickly.

The only true feral she has ever seen, says Karen, is one of the Homeless Eight of Brocton. She was a big, long-haired black and white female cat, who wouldn't let any humans near her, let alone touch her. She wasn't too fond of other cats either, and luckily found a home on a farm owned by a gentleman farmer. There were just a few animals at the farm, but he wanted cats in the barn.

Based on her considerable experience of dealing with feral cats, Karen actually describes them as semi-feral. These are the ferals who have lived in the wild but can be socialized to become friendly and learn to live with humans. Feral kittens can be tamed every time and adopted, and some adults too can be turned or flipped. This is another cause that's dear to Karen's heart and if she can flip a semi-feral cat and find it a home, she will do so rather than release it back into the wild.

Karen's experience bears out what feline advocates have been seeing, as TNR programs expand across the US. Local shelters see a sharp drop in intakes within a year or two when TNR programs are started in any area. It also means a better quality of life for those cats that are finally released back, since they have also been vaccinated and given any medical treatments necessary. Alley Cat Allies is one of the national organizations that has pioneered TNR, beginning with the community cats of the Atlantic City Boardwalk. These cats have become a tourist attraction in their own right. A dedicated group of volunteers, supported by local businesses, makes sure the cats are always fed and cared for and that they have shelter from cold and stormy weather.

Despite the success stories, TNR faces strong opposition from the authorities in many locations, which specifically prohibit feline advocates from trapping and fixing cats. State parks, local municipalities and others have an inordinate amount of power to limit the activities of community cat advocates. This can be and has been changed through advocacy with local elected representatives, but there's still a lot of work to be done in this regard. Advocacy at the local and state levels may be the way forward to support efforts to better the lives of community cats.

––––

What makes TNR so urgent is that it also offers the best chance of stopping the annual holocaust of dogs and cats carried out by way of "euthanization" at overfull shelters. The last time a survey on number of "euthanizations" was done back in 1998, it found that over four and a half million dogs and cats were killed by the people charged with protecting them. With the trend towards no-kill shelters, the numbers have gone down to some extent, but remain upwards of two million a year. The expansion of TNR programs could put an end to this horrendous level of institutionalized cruelty.

Life for feral cats is difficult and dangerous, which is another reason why TNR becomes a matter of urgency. I've often wondered if cats can survive in the wild, on their own. A lost, stray or homeless cat in a built environment is going to get into trouble sooner or later, but what about cats living in the woods and fields? Can they live wild? As a novice cat owner nearly thirty years ago, I had bought every book on cat care I could find. Those glossy productions by self- styled experts assured me that seemingly domesticated tabbies were really wild creatures at heart. At the back of my mind, there always lurked the fear and guilt that by giving cats a home, I was depriving them of their rightful existence in the wild. Not so.

Karen tells me that cats are ingenious, resourceful and real survivors, but they're not wild animals. They're adaptable and can suffer through and survive in the wild, but it's very dangerous for them. In the woods, they're at a disadvantage because they're low in the food chain. Adult cats can climb trees to escape predators, but kittens are very vulnerable even to low-level predators like possum and raccoon. Cats living on their own in the wild have a harder life and a lower life expectancy. They're also vulnerable to all kinds of human cruelty and the story of the feral cats from North East is told in Chapter 8. Cats made their choice and became domestic animals long ago, giving up their wildness to become our companions. It's up to us to keep our side of the compact.

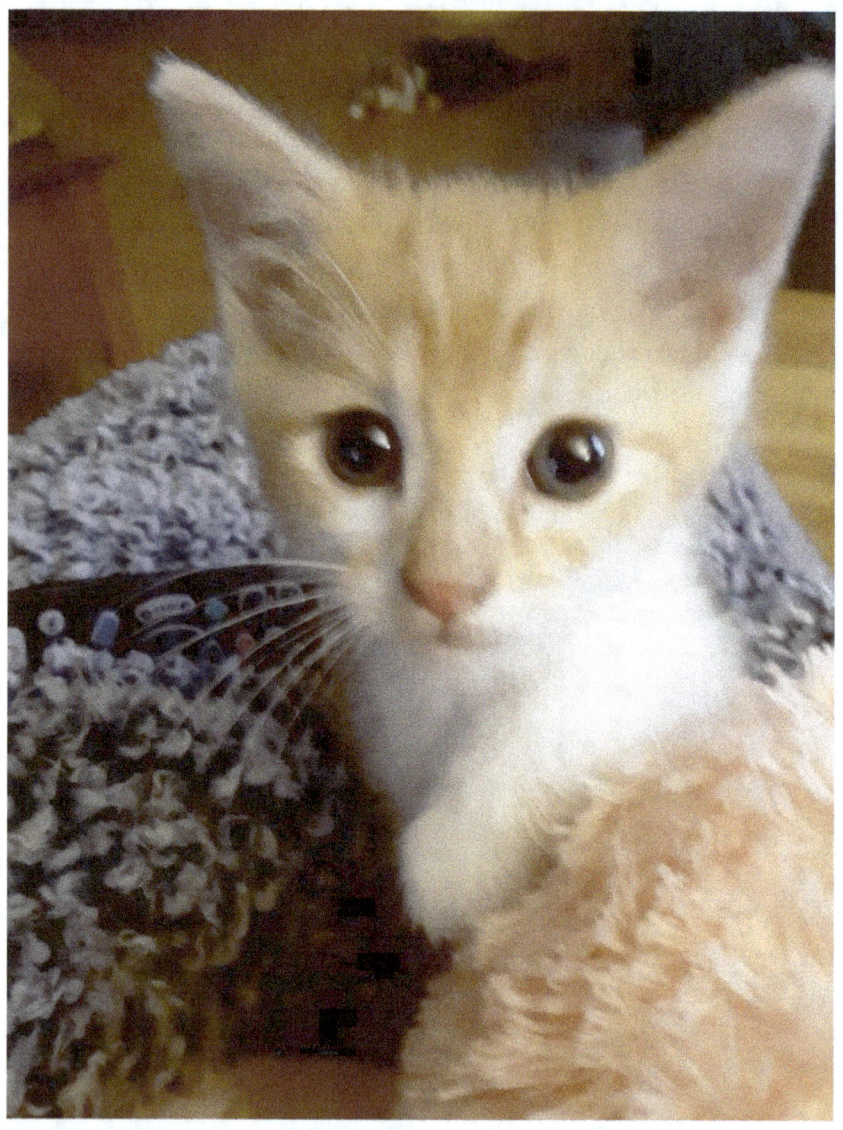

Otto as a kitten. He was one of Karen's feral rescues from Ripley who flipped and became tame.

8

Cruelty and Kindness

One of the great mysteries of cat rescue is the juxtaposition of human cruelty and kindness. Sometimes cats have just wandered into trouble and gotten trapped, injured or otherwise harmed. And at other times, they are the targets of deliberate human cruelty, which can take many different forms, from the kitten left by the roadside with her feet tied in duct tape to cats and kittens abandoned in the woods by owners, or even worse. We are learning more and more about how cruelty to animals easily segues into violence against humans as well.

The National Sheriffs' Association (NSA) sees it as a 'gateway crime' linked to other forms of criminal activity including domestic violence, child abuse, homicide, drug and weapons violations and more. The NSA in fact played a leading role in advocating for the FBI to track animal cruelty crimes. In 2016, the FBI added animal cruelty as a distinct crime to its National Incident-Based Reporting System (NIBRS). This recognizes, on the basis of years of empirical evidence, that there is no dividing line between abuse of animals and abuse of humans.

As information from the database becomes available, it is expected that patterns linking animal cruelty with other crimes will emerge, emphasizing the need for action to prevent cruelty and mistreatment of animals.

Researchers are already identifying animal abuse as not only a gateway crime but also as a red flag for other kinds of abuse. A 2021 article by Charlie Robinson and Victoria Clausen highlights the findings of FBI animal cruelty investigators: "Animal cruelty is a predictor of current and future violence, including crimes of assault, rape, murder, arson, domestic violence and sexual abuse of children. Further, animal cruelty is a better predictor of sexual abuse compared to a history of homicide, arson, or weapon convictions. Being cognizant of this link allows for law enforcement to recognize that animal cruelty indicates other possible offenses are occurring in the household."

For us as individuals, almost the hardest part is to see the animals, in their innocence, deal with the effects of cruelty. They can never tell us what they've been through, like the beautiful black cat belonging to one of my former neighbors. She had just shown up at his house and he took her in. His house was known locally as one that would not turn away a stray or homeless cat, so people dropped off unwanted cats in the vicinity and the cats found their way to his house. Molly was one of those. She loved being patted, but each time a human reached out a hand to her, she would recoil and cringe. As did a dog I met at another farm, who had been handed on by a previous owner, where he had probably been mistreated. The dog, too, loved to be patted but cringed every time a human hand went near his neck or throat.

For rescuers, the contrast between the grace and innocence of the animals and the suffering they have gone through can be heartbreaking.

Especially when the suffering is caused by other humans. It takes a special kind of courage to persist in the mission of rescue in the face of all the accumulated weight of cruelty. The random nature of cruelty, deriving from the kind of power that humans have over the lives of animals, can be frightening in itself. That's the story of the feral cat colony living on the lot next to the Freeport Restaurant in North East, PA, just across the New York State line from Chautauqua County. Diana Seman, who worked at the restaurant, had been feeding them for twelve years. And then one day, suddenly and without giving any reason, the owner of the property told Diana that she had to stop feeding the cats and stop entering the lot. The cats had to go, she said, and the lot was posted. Diana got in touch with Karen and WSCR and they went out to try and trap the ferals to rescue them. Another rescue group in Erie also tried to rescue the cats, but there wasn't enough time to get them all.

It takes days to humanely trap a number of cats and the owner refused to give them any time. They asked her to give them just one month to get all the cats off the property. At first, she agreed and then, abruptly, changed her mind. Karen and WSCR managed to rescue some of the ferals and the group from Erie got a few. But just a couple of days later, people saw a truck roll onto the property, full of traps and cages. It drove away a few hours later and the cats were gone. Roscoe and Kit, mentioned in Chapter 3, were among those rescued near Freeport Restaurant. Hoot, a striking tortoiseshell with kittens, was also rescued there and was adopted by Karen and her husband.

————

Pennsylvania state laws on animal cruelty protect domestic animals from mistreatment. Domestic animals are defined as "Any dog, cat, equine animal, bovine animal, sheep, goat or porcine animal." This definition depends on species rather than ownership and covers feral cats. The state criminal statutes define animal cruelty as a criminal act. According to 18 Pa.C.S.A. § 5511. Cruelty to animals (2.1) (i), "A person commits a misdemeanor of the first degree if he willfully and maliciously, (A) maims, mutilates, tortures or disfigures any dog or cat, whether belonging to himself or otherwise."

In both New York and Pennsylvania states, a first offense of animal cruelty is defined as a misdemeanor, like domestic assault. A repeat crime turns into a felony with more serious penalties. Under the current animal cruelty laws in New York State, it is illegal to hurt cats, even if they are strays or if they belong to other people, even if found on your property. In other words, the legal protections against animal cruelty apply to all cats and other domestic animals. They are species-wide and not dependent on their status as pets or strays.

While the laws are sound, the difficult part is enforcement. It's not easy to catch animal abusers in the act and even harder to find evidence that will stand in court. And in a rural area like Chautauqua County, ASPCA doesn't have the resources and manpower to monitor reports of abuse in all the far-flung and remote areas. Some localities like Chautauqua County are also setting up public databases of known animal abusers, on the model of child abuser registries. This would prevent stores from selling animals to individuals on the registry, but these projects are still in their early stages. At present Tennessee is the only state that has a statewide animal abuser registry.

Where do kindness and cruelty come from? Everyone has their own horror stories of animal abuse. What makes one person feed sixty to seventy cats for years, while another just decides to destroy with an entire colony of feral cats? These are immediate questions that cat rescuers face every day. Judy is appalled at the things that people can do, like setting a cat on fire. She and Celeste both feel that cruelty is learned in families and that the way to counter it is through education that inculcates love and respect for nature.

Celeste's concerns for abandoned cats and kittens struck a chord for me because it was when I was trying to find homes for abandoned kittens that I first encountered Karen and WSCR. It was the end of my first summer in Chautauqua. I was staying on a farm and my landlord saw an abandoned kitten at the edge of the woods a few miles away. He told me I might want to go rescue it and bring it back since he knew I loved cats. It turned out that there was not just one kitten, but five, all of whom needed homes. Re- reading a story I wrote at that time about our rescue operation, I realized that it was also a story about the courage of cats left to die. And about the heartbreaking juxtaposition of cruelty and kindness that is part of animal rescue. Part of that story is reproduced here because it connects to this one. I had found two kittens, who were too small or too weak to run and seen two more.

"Before heading back to the farm with the first two, I stopped at the house nearby to make sure they weren't pets. No one was home, but at the next house, they said the kittens had been there for four or five days. Four or five days in the 90-degree weather without food or water and no one had thought to help them or even call the SPCA.

Back at the farm, we pulled out all the cans of tuna we could find. Even before going back for the other two, I had to feed the tiger striped and small black ones. Though tiny, they were able to eat solid food and between them polished off one whole can of tuna. The small black kitten then went to sleep with her chin resting on the dish that had contained the first food she'd eaten for five days.

In the meantime, a neighbor had arrived with her cat carrier and her van to help bring back the other two. The white kitten came for the tuna, but Patch ran around for a while, before deciding to let me pick him up to join his sister. Four kittens, instead of one. The farmhouse was already bursting at the seams with four people, two kids, two dogs, a barn cat and a house cat, to say nothing of the cows and chickens and guinea hens. But the house have never turned away anyone in need.

The kittens were put in the only room in the house with a door, to stop them from straying. Especially the tiger striped one, who mewed at me till he lost his little voice and kept climbing all over trying to go - where? What did he want? He was fed and had a place to sleep, his brother and sisters around him, no visible injuries. And he still kept on mewing, though no sound came out.

Another neighbor brought a box of food and took away three kittens to foster. By now we were desperately calling every shelter we could find a phone number for, only to get answering machines telling us they were full. I made a quick dash to the grocery store, a chance to pick up more cat food and take stock of the situation. But it was difficult to think straight. I was haunted by the image of tiny pointy ears in the roadside grass and expected to find abandoned kittens along every verge. The cruelty behind the action was almost mind-destroying.

For no good reason, on my way home, with dusk closing in, I drove back out to the dirt road and the woods. The moon was shining high above the trees, lighting my way. And there he was, on the other side of the road! The fifth kitten, who had hidden in the woods that morning, which was why I had missed him. By now, left all alone, he wanted to be found, was bouncing around the roadside, saying, "Mee! Mee! You left Mee behind, pick Mee up! Take Mee Home!" So that was what Tiger had been trying to tell me.

The moon and the forest protected the kittens from heat and hunger and thirst and all the dangers of the wilds. In mortal peril, the kittens kept together and looked out for each other. At the farm, the little grey barn cat and the little black farmhouse cat watched over them and played with them and helped them recover from their ordeal.

To cut a long story short, we found homes for all of them. The neighbor kept Tiger. The farmer found a friend to adopt the white girl cat. Patch and Simon (the fifth kitten) were taken by Lakeshore SPCA in Dunkirk and immediately adopted to a loving home. And the smallest one, the little black kitten, was taken by the Westfield Stray Cat Rescue, even though they had no room. A beautiful, kind woman called Karen took her home to foster.

These were not feral kittens, who might even have been able to fend for themselves, left in the wild. They were socialized, friendly to humans and completely at the mercy of the elements. What kind of person would leave them there to die? And not just once, but every year? Later that year, in September, after I had left, they found two more abandoned in front of the neighbor's home, thrown out of a car that didn't even stop. They took them in and found them homes.

I went back the next summer and every day feared to find abandoned kittens by the roadside. But that year there was only one, white with orange patches and she came walking along the road to a neighbor's house, footsore and exhausted. He brought her to the farm, and we took her in. The Westfield Stray Cat Rescue was full up again, but they paid for her medical treatment. She had walked a long way and there were tiny pebbles embedded in her paws, which were swollen and had running sores. Just when I was about to despair of being able to help her, Karen of WSCR called me and offered to care for her.

There were many theories about who might abandon kittens on that road year after year. Someone who visited the area regularly but didn't live there? Someone who hunted in the area? A nearby farm with an overpopulation of cats, resorting to traditional means such as abandonment or drowning of kittens? Someone who had access to a seemingly regular supply of kittens? I don't know if it is a crime, in the eyes of the law, to abandon kittens to die. But it should be.

I haven't gone back to Chautauqua this year. But if there might be cruel humans leaving kittens to die, there are also kind humans rescuing them and giving them loving homes."

The story about the little orange and white cat with the sore paws has an even happier ending. Karen healed him (he turned out to be a boy) and kept him. Rhett has grown up into a beautiful, gentle and "unassuming" cat.

———

Hoarding cats and other animals is a different kind of story. Even though it's portrayed in the media as animal cruelty with images of scores and even hundreds of animals kept in miserable conditions, it may start out as an act of kindness that gets out of hand. It can just start with someone who can't turn away homeless animals that show up or are dropped off by people. Without meaning any harm, the numbers grow to the point that there is no more money for medical needs or to spay and neuter. And it goes downhill from there. Is there a better way to handle the problem than to sensationalize it as animal cruelty and criminalize the person?

A kinder way to deal with the problem can be seen in Westfield's good hoarding story, about a gentleman called Harlee who had around fifteen cats. There were two mother cats with eight kittens between them, two teens and two to three more adult cats. Harlee was aware that the numbers were more than he could handle, and he contacted Karen and WSCR to help him find homes for some of the cats. Karen contacted the Chautauqua County Humane in Jamestown and they agreed to take the mothers; the kittens went to foster homes. All the adult cats were also spayed and neutered.

But Harlee had a hard time giving them up and Karen remembers that he would often change his mind when she went to his home to pick up the cats. "You had to be ready to get them on the day he was amenable to giving them up," she says, "because waiting until the next day might be too late. He might have changed his mind overnight." Because this tendency to hoard was caught in time, it ended happily. After he passed away, his girlfriend asked Karen to help find homes for the remaining cats. She lived in an apartment with three cats of her own and had no room for any more.

————

Cats are capable of incredible acts of kindness to their people, to other cats and to other creatures. This is something every cat owner knows. Cats know when you're feeling down and will cheer you up, by sitting in your lap and purring or chasing around the house with their madcap antics. As I discovered with the kittens abandoned in the woods, they will look out for each other.

And then there are the famous and less well-known stories. There was Scarlett, the mother cat who rescued her kittens from a fire in Brooklyn, going back into the burning building five times to bring each one out, even though she suffered terrible burns. By the time she got them all out, she couldn't see, because of the condition of her eyes. She did a head count by nosing the kittens, to make sure all were safe, before collapsing. A firefighter took her to the North Shore Animal League and she and her kittens found kind homes. There's Street Cat Bob who helped author James Bowen fight drug addiction and turn his life around. There was the small black cat and dog found wandering by the roadside in Waterford, Ireland, with burn injuries. They had kept each other company through their ordeals and refused to be separated, crying piteously when shelter workers tried to put them in different areas for cats and dogs. They were adopted together.

Karen says in her experience, a nursing mother cat will adopt an orphaned kitten that needs to feed, every single time. She has never known a mother cat to refuse a kitten that needed a mother. While scientists might rationalize this as a response to a deeply rooted biological mother instinct, rather than an altruistic choice, the truth is that cats are smart enough to know their own kittens from another cat's. And according to the scientific calculus of survival, they should refuse to feed them, saving the nourishment for their own kittens. But instead, defying science and 'instinct,' they adopt and rear orphans, every single time.

Karen tells me about Misty, who was a very feral tabby cat. She was one of those rescued from the lot behind the Freeport Restaurant in North East and wouldn't let any humans near her. She was nursing her own kittens at a foster home. A motherless kitten was brought in at the time, in need of a foster mother. Misty was not at all friendly to people but when Karen held out the orphan kitten to her, she just reached out a paw and drew the kitten in to start feeding. She brought it up along with her own. As Karen told the story, I had no doubt at all that this was about Misty choosing to nurse and rear the kitten: a moral and intelligent creature making a moral and intelligent choice. Misty's kittens all found good homes and Misty herself went to live on a farm.

Fairy tales are full of animal guardians, helpers and protectors, who help humans find their way through bad luck and enmity, sometimes at the cost of their own lives. Science and modernity turned this relationship into a story about domestication and animal friends into the servants of humankind or even worse, into our chattels. As we are forced in this age of anthropogenic environmental devastation to rethink our relationship to the world of nature, maybe the cats have something to teach us.

Simon, the fifth kitten

9

Volunteers and Fosters

Shelter volunteers are a special group, and their love and dedication can be seen in the demeanor of the cats they care for. Cats don't give their trust lightly, nor should they. But at WSCR, they know they're safe. No matter whose shift it is, Ramona, Tami, Jessica, Denise or anyone else, the cats will be looked after, fed and watered, their litter boxes and condos cleaned and there's always time for games and hugs as well. The volunteers are highly motivated and self- directed, working efficiently as a team to keep things running smoothly. Many will stop by to help out or just to say hello to the cats even on days they're not officially working at the shelter. Tami even brings her little dog along for the day and he has an extra bed in the sorting room at the store. He gets along with the cats and generally is good as gold. Ramona is another dedicated volunteer who has been working at the shelter and store for years, finding time even when her own cat was ill.

The youngest volunteer, Wyatt, is eleven years old. He comes to the shelter with his mother and his favorite part is socializing the cats, he says. He's very good at it. The littlest kitten, tiny CC who was fostered and eventually adopted by Celeste, was in the store that day for her weekly visit and the two are the best of friends. Wyatt, too, knows to hold the kitten against his heart, where she feels safe. He's on equally good terms with the adult cats and expertly carried around the large black cat who was visiting another day.

The shelter also gets a lot of volunteers from the local high school, because students have to do a certain number of hours of community service to graduate. The Westfield Academy Volunteer Experience or WAVE program teaches kids how important it is to give back to the community. It works out very well, Karen says, and it's nice to see how good the kids are with the cats. The people and cats at WSCR are teaching the children well.

All WSCR staff are volunteers. Denise Spencer is the WSCR Treasurer and accountant. She works full time and has two kids but finds the time to handle all the paperwork and keeps it all in order. She maintains proper records and makes sure the bills get paid on time. She also volunteers a full day at The Thrifty Kitty, using up her only weekday off from work.

Many of the volunteers and staff, like Karen and Celeste, also foster cats and kittens. Judy Loomis, though no longer actively involved with the shelter, was looking after a basket of kittens someone brought in, until there was room for them at the Chautauqua County Humane Shelter in Jamestown. Celeste's specialty and her particular talent, is in looking after cats who have special medical needs and also mother cats with nursing kittens. She tells me about one cat who came in with a dreadful injury from having gotten his front leg caught in his collar. The collar had cut deeply into the skin and had to be cut away. The wound underneath was very raw and needed careful cleaning and medication to prevent infection. Dr. Rogers did not want to suture it but left it open to heal. Celeste had to apply an antibiotic solution to the wound and to keep it clean, both very difficult tasks. Dr. Rogers was very pleased with the way it healed, she recalled, and the cat recovered fully.

How did she learn to care for sick cats? "Vets are the best teachers," she says, and Dr. Rogers would explain everything he was doing when he treated the cats. That training has helped save many cats. Infections, worms, sores, broken bones and eye surgery - Celeste has helped cats recover from all of these and go on to live happy lives.

Celeste also remembered Georgie with love and sadness, a cat who was too badly injured to survive. He had been shot, possibly with an arrow, and had a wound that needed to be drained on both sides of his body. He was starved, with the bones of his spine growing out of the skin. The wound developed an infection that took his life, but in the time he was with her, the small black cat was so gentle and loving that losing him was a great sadness. She says she has learned to accept the losses. Sometimes the cats come in from such desperate situations, that all that can be done is to make them comfortable. This caring might even give them the best days of their hard lives.

Celeste has the greatest admiration for the way that Karen will stay with cats till the very end and especially when they have to be euthanized. Karen says that for reasons that she doesn't quite understand, she wants them to know they are not alone when they are sick or at the end of their lives. Cats may have a parallel instinct. I was reminded of a story I heard years ago from my cat sitter in Brooklyn, Gilda Provenzano. She was looking after my cat Nuffy, who was then a small scruffy black kitten. She spent more on toys and treats for him than she charged for cat sitting while I traveled for a fevered round of conferences and job interviews. I was just learning about the magic of black cats and Gilda had plenty of black cat stories. She told me about the 18-year-old black cat who had lived at her yoga studio. One night he passed away peacefully in his sleep. They found him the next morning curled up to the Buddha statue in the studio, hugging it with his arms. I've never been able to answer the question that stays with me since hearing this story: was it the human or the divine that he found in the statue?

Karen herself got involved with WSCR when she and her family moved back to Ripley after a long time. She has always had cats and remembers Boots, a black and white cat, who was her childhood pet. She started coming to WSCR with her son because she wanted him to be involved with volunteer work. Working with cats was something they both enjoyed. Along with Celeste, she specializes in fostering cats that are injured or sick and need special medical care. In fact, both have turned part of their homes into intensive care units for cats.

I got to meet one of the sick cats Karen was caring for, a beautiful young longhair with white and dark tabby patches. Hobo had just been abandoned near her house one evening. A couple of months later, he was suffering from undiagnosed health problems. Strongly articulating a feeling that many pet owners have had, Karen says that she doesn't like to leave cats overnight at the veterinary clinic, where they will be alone. So she learned how to give Hobo subcutaneous fluids in lieu of an IV drip and took him home with her. Since he needed to be watched and fed regularly, he went to the office with her too and slept contentedly while she handled phone calls, adoptions and my questions. Sadly, Hobo passed away on a Saturday morning, December 17, 2016, at 4 a.m. He was at home with Karen and her family, surrounded by love.

Karen is also one of the fosters who specializes in fostering orphaned kittens. When they're very tiny, they have to be fed every two hours. With the multiple demands on her time, with family, church and WSCR commitments, Karen got into the habit of bringing along the kittens with her in the car. They go everywhere with her, to stores, restaurants and on one memorable occasion, to a doctor's appointment with her husband. They travel in a purse-sized bag and are not often noticed. But if they are, the cuteness factor overwhelms any objections and Karen has never faced any problems in bringing them with her wherever she goes.

Marissa, who came to be known as Puck, was one of those kittens. The little black kitten came to the shelter from her foster home when she was old enough, but at the age of about 12-15 weeks, she got sick and had to be taken home to be cared for. Caring for Puck meant force-feeding her every two hours. With her busy schedule, it was impossible for Karen to go back home at short intervals, so she decided to take the cat with her instead. Puck went everywhere with Karen, even to Max's high school hockey games. The small black kitten became the team mascot and regularly went to the ice hockey arena to watch the team play. And that was how she came to be called Puck.

Puck is now grown up, but she still loves to ride in the car and go to the drive-in theater, to restaurants and the shops. Her comments on humans and their preoccupations are pure feline delight. At the drive-in theater in Erie, she says, "Yeah, Dad, we come here all the time, but I see the same movie every time: bright lights, stupid people." She goes to the Pet Smart as well, which welcomes pets of all kinds, though it's rare to see cats there. Puck's sandwich choices are simple: "Can you get me a…a…a…salami samwich? Just the salami, Mom, skip the bread!" She had a good week Christmas shopping recently.

Cats get up to all kinds of mischief and in a house full of cats, there's never a dull moment. Two of Karen's fosters, shy ones who liked to hide, did it so successfully that they vanished from sight for a long time. She left food and water for them at their approximate locations, and it was clear that they were eating regularly and using their litter boxes, which she kept clean. But they managed to stay out of sight for weeks and even months. Joby was a tiny kitten being kept in a bathroom to separate him from other cats. Finding the door to the closet under the sink open, he managed to squeeze through a hole in the wall at the back and hide in the space behind. After an initial panic and search in the small, enclosed space, Karen and her family figured that he must be inside the wall behind the sink. She could reach in with a camera phone and take a picture, which showed him sitting there snugly, inside the wall behind the closet. He was too far in to be caught and refused to come out. So he was left there, with food and water and clean litter in the bathroom. He stayed in hiding for two weeks before Karen finally live trapped him, in the bathroom.

Attica, who truly earned her name, was another shy cat who was being kept separate in Karen's home office. She managed to slip through the door into the adjoining attic and vanished from sight for two whole months. She would come out when no one was around, to eat and drink water and use the litter box. Until one day, two months later, when Karen was replenishing her food bowl and heard a "Mew!" behind her. And there was Attica, ready to rejoin the world. Both Joby and Attica found good homes.

Is it difficult to give up the fosters? Many people end up adopting their first fosters. Giving up fosters is a mixture of sadness and joy. They are missed, Karen says, but there is the happiness of knowing that they will be well looked after. And having the space opens the way to helping other cats in need.

Animal rescue can be exhausting work, physically, financially and emotionally. Rescue and shelter workers have to perform miracles in continuous crisis mode, with very little support, which is why they often burn out. They are moved to act by their conscience and their only reward is being able to help an animal in need. It's what keeps them going. In Karen's case, there's a strong spirit of determination, and "I've got this" attitude and a sense of fun she shares with the cats and other animals. It has helped over a thousand cats survive and that is equally inspiring to other people as well.

There have been times when larger rescue organizations couldn't make a start on problems too large to handle, but Karen and WSCR found a way. A few years ago in Dunkirk, a death in the family became an emergency for the cats. This is a very common situation and family members find themselves unable to care for the cats suddenly left without an owner. WSCR was contacted by a man whose mother had passed away. When he came in to close up her apartment, he discovered that she had 22 cats, comfortably housed in the basement, but now suddenly there was no one to care for them. He reached out to local rescue organizations for help, but initially, the larger groups were paralyzed by the scale of rescue that was needed, Karen organized teams of volunteers to go in twice a day to feed and care for the cats until homes or fosters could be found for them. As Karen began finding fosters for the cats, Lakeshore Humane in Dunkirk and the Chautauqua County Humane Society began to take in a few as well.

Karen modestly attributes her success to the ability to look at any task and break it down into manageable components. What others can see and respond to is her inspiring example and cheerful spirit, which helps them to keep going when they feel discouraged. Cats are very discerning people and there's no doubt that they pick their rescuers and champions. Even if health problems prevent Karen from continuing a grueling schedule of rescue and shelter work, her knowledge, practical experience and above all, indomitable spirit should continue to serve as a guide. Perhaps education and advocacy are two channels to communicate these to a larger audience.

Time does not stand still, and change is the only constant. Between the time I finished writing the manuscript and its publication, a great deal has happened at WSCR. Due to ill health, Karen has stepped back from her commitments at the shelter. This means that WSCR has also had to scale back its work and limit intake to a number that can be housed at the shelter alone. The pandemic too has forced WSCR to make many changes in its operations, though things are slowly returning to normal. Karen continues to look after stray cats and other creatures at her home, in the house and in the outdoor shelter. All of them are healthy, happy and well-cared for and loved as individuals.

Luckily for the cats of Chautauqua County and those who love them, there are plenty of people looking out for them, in the real world and online. The Internet is a great place for cat videos, of course, which evolve into international online communities of cat lovers. Social media, though much vilified (and much of the criticism is well deserved) has the potential to unite for good as much as it can divide. Anything that brings together people from such varied locations as Thailand, Japan, China, Brazil, Malaysia, Norway, Turkey, Russia and the US, competing for the wittiest responses to funny cat pictures and videos, has to be a good thing. At the local level, it helps to link up communities to watch for lost and missing pets and to help reunite them with their people.

Chautauqua County has a large number of online lost and found cat communities. Some of the pictures and descriptions of missing cats are truly heartrending and touching, showing just how much the furry little beasts are loved. Online communities sharing information about lost pets help to dramatically improve their chances of reuniting with their people.

Social media also highlight the work of small, local rescues and shelters and individuals who do feline rescue quietly and off the grid as it were. Chautauqua has its share of such helpers and healers as well who use their own funds to shelter and care for stray, lost and injured cats who have nowhere else to go. Small rescue groups like the Little Angels Animal Sanctuary and Sherman Community Pet Project rely on community support for their work, which is mainly TVNR, emergency rescue and re-homing felines. They don't have a lot of funding or recognition from official sources, but what drives them is concern and empathy for the stray cats lost and wandering in a dangerous world.

Nap time at Hubbard House

10

The Road Ahead

What does the future hold for WSCR? For Karen, it's important to be able to sustain the work, to find those who will continue it and to hand over to them a rescue organization that's as stable as possible. What would the cats say to her? She says that cats are amazingly adaptable and have the ability to roll with the punches. Their advice might well be to not worry so much because things will work out. Things have a way of working out.

Celeste's hope for the future is that WSCR will continue to evolve and meet new challenges, as it has done for the first ten years of its existence. Judy's wish is a simple one: she looks forward to the day that there will be no more need for shelters like WSCR, because there will be no more cruelty to cats and other animals and there will be no more strays in need of help.

There is a message for all of us, perhaps specially for those concerned with education and policy-making, on how to shape a future that has more kindness than cruelty. Good laws can help, but they can only go so far. Education is the key to reaching much further, in space as well as in time. People who are on the frontlines of animal rescue, like Karen and others in Chautauqua County, around the US and indeed around the world, have a unique perspective and experience that needs a wider hearing.

With all its faults, the Internet has taken cats to its heart worldwide and offers an interesting path to the future. Besides the obligatory cute cat videos, which we can never get enough of, online cat communities are slowly starting to realize their potential for other causes like search and rescue, fundraising and giving a platform to smaller shelters to connect to both local and worldwide communities. Thanks to social media, cat people around the world, in locations as diverse as Turkey, the UK, Malaysia, Russia, Mexico and Norway, to name just a few, can learn from each other's experiences and of course, share cute cat pictures in different cultural settings. As in so many other things, the Internet has already started to level the playing field, removing the sting of casual insults bestowed on crazy cat ladies and on cats themselves. It's a path that feline advocates can use to move beyond medieval and contemporary ailurophobic tropes to gain recognition of the richness that cats add to our lives.

What do the cats make of them and the WSCR? Celeste feels that cats are honest, while dogs will be subservient to their human owners. Many a cat owner may have wondered what their cat thinks about them and then figured they're better off not knowing. But the cats do have an answer and at WSCR it can be seen in the serenity and trust with which they greet their humans. Their unbroken spirit, full of dignity and playfulness, despite the harsh suffering they have gone through, is a lesson that we might learn.

Those in need of help can be human as well as feline. Karen recalls that recently she received a phone call from Judith, who feeds the ferals in Brocton and who helped WSCR with the Homeless Eight. They talked for a long time, but when they finally hung up, Karen's daughter, who was visiting, said "You didn't talk about cats at all!" Karen realized that was true; Judith was upset about something and just needed someone to talk things through. This story resonates with my own experience.

There aren't too many precise dates in this story. But right in the beginning, November 4, 2016, wrote itself in as a section heading in the first chapter. It was the first time I sat down with Karen to talk about the book and that conversation became the foundation for this book. The previous day I had lost a cat, who was too badly injured to survive. She was an unknown tiger tabby and I found her near an electric fence on the farm in Forestville. The cat, who turned out to be stray or lost, was mewing in distress and was paralyzed from the neck down. As soon I picked her up, she stopped crying and started purring instead. I took her indoors and quickly gave her some dry food. She purred as she ate a little. Putting her in an improvised carrier, made with a borrowed laundry basket and towels, I drove her to the nearest vet. They treated it as an emergency and did all they could to stabilize her. She was kept at the clinic overnight and seemed to improve by evening, eating and even trying to sit up.

The next day, however, it went downhill and by afternoon she was gone. It was a devastating story I had experienced before, a beautiful magical creature in a beautiful magical place, struck down by misfortune. We never found out who she was, or even what happened to her: the vet ruled out electrocution and most types of poisoning. But in the very brief time I and the clinic staff interacted with her, she won our hearts with her gentleness and grace. At least, at the end, she was not alone but surrounded by people who loved her and wanted to help.

The following day, I met Karen at the Thrifty Kitty. She knew about the cat and was deeply sympathetic, with her profound knowledge of what was involved emotionally. As Fallon watched over us, Karen talked to me for nearly four hours, our conversation punctuated by phone calls, an adoption and visits from various volunteers, including the youngest. By evening, I had a story and a purpose. She had talked me through the loss.

————

In difficult economic times, cat rescues see an increasing number of surrendered and abandoned animals. The numbers don't tell the story of the anguish suffered by people and pets alike who are caught up in such harsh choices. Looking at the large number of posts on social media desperately seeking homes for pets whose people can no longer afford to keep them, it becomes clear that human and animal woes are closely connected. And conversely, so are human and animal welfare. It becomes necessary to state this because so many environmentalists tend to leave animals and especially domestic pets out of the vision for repairing the harm humans have done to the natural world. A world that works for cats would be a world that works for humans as well.

Completing the Circle is a story I read a long time ago, in elementary school in India. A story from the life of the Buddha when he was a boy called Siddhartha. It goes like this:

Siddhartha and his cousin Devadutta, who features in Buddhist texts as the Buddha's evil adversary and tormentor in later life, were playing in the garden when they saw a flight of swans in the sky.

Quickly, Devadutta strung an arrow to his bow and shot, with deadly accuracy. An injured bird fell to earth. Its wing was broken, and Siddhartha took it away to care for it. Once the bird was healed, Devadutta came to claim it as his property. "It was my arrow that brought it down," he said, "the bird belongs to me."

"But I was the one who healed it," said Siddhartha, "and saved its life."

The argument continued and eventually, it was brought before the sages. Their judgement was: the bird would decide. So the two cousins were placed twenty paces apart in the great hall and the bird was set down exactly in between. Without hesitating, the bird walked straight to Siddhartha. He took it to the garden and set it free.

And from a completely different place and culture, is a song inspired by the Prayer of St. Francis of Assisi, by Irish singer and songwriter Moya Brennan. Titled 'Peacemaker,' it is sung and spoken in English and Gaelic, by Brennan and her son Paul, who was four years old when the song was recorded in 1999:
"Make me a channel of Your peace…
If you give love You will receive love And it is by dying
One awakens to eternal life.
Where there is hatred, I bring love.
Lord, guide us."
The great mystery of life itself is the interweaving of hurt and healing, beauty and fear, grief and courage. The opposites are inescapable, but we can always choose kindness and hope.

The Christmas Store December 2016